YOU, INC.

Burke Hedges

*I know of no more encouraging fact
than the unquestionable ability
of man to elevate his life
by conscious endeavor.*
— Henry David Thoreau

inti

Publishing

You, Inc.

*10 Simple Principles to Dramatically
Increase Your Fair Market Value!*

By Burke Hedges

Printed in the United States of America
First Edition, October, 1996

ISBN 0-9632667-3-x

Published by INTI Publishing
Tampa, FL

(813) 881-1638
E-MAIL: intipub@worldnet.att.net
Website: http://www.intipub.com

Cover Design by The Jenkins Group
Layout by Bayou Graphics

ALSO BY BURKE HEDGES
• • •

Who Stole the American Dream?

You Can't Steal Second with Your Foot on First!

Copycat Marketing 101

YOU, INC. Audio Series
(6 audio cassettes and workbook)

For more information on books and tapes available
through INTI Publishing, visit our online bookstore:
http://www.intipub.com

CONTENTS
· · ·

SECTION 1:
Introduction

SECTION 2:
10 Simple Principles to Dramatically Increase Your Fair Market Value!

SECTION 3:
Conclusion

DEDICATION

• • •

This book is dedicated to YOU ... for having the wisdom to understand that the door to self-improvement only opens from within.

SECTION 1

• • •

Introduction:
Think — YOU, INC.!

Inherently, each one of us has the substance within to achieve whatever our goals and dreams define. What is missing from each of us is the training, education, knowledge, and insight to use what we already have.

— Mark Twain

INTRODUCTION:
Think — YOU, INC.!

You are NOT what you think you are.
But what you think — YOU ARE!

— Dr. Norman Vincent Peale

Many years ago an auctioneer was selling off the estate of a wealthy industrialist.

As the auction came to a close, the tired auctioneer held up a dusty, discolored old violin and asked mockingly, *"What am I bid for this? ... $100 ... no takers? ... Do I hear $75? ... $50? ... $25? $5?*

"How about a dollar?" he implored, as the audience's laughter echoed around the empty walls.

A faint, cracked voice interrupted the laughter. *"Excuse me. May I have a moment of your time?"*

A bent old man shuffled up to the auctioneer and reached for the violin with a thin pale hand. With his back to the audience, the old man plucked each string and expertly adjusted the tuning pegs. Slowly turning to the audience, he motioned for silence ... and then placing the violin gently under his chin, he began to play.

Lovely, clear notes filled the room, and the audience sat frozen with awe as the old man serenaded them with a heavenly solo. When the solo ended, the old man bowed deeply at the waist ... handed the violin to the auctioneer ... and walked slowly out the door as everyone burst into spontaneous applause.

The smiling auctioneer held up the old violin and shouted above the noisy crowd, *"Now what am I bid for this MOST EXTRAORDINARY instrument? A thousand to the man in the top hat ... I hear two thousand from the woman in the front ... Back to the gentleman ... three thousand,* *you say? ... Do I hear four? ... Four it is! Do I hear five thousand? Five it is! ... Five going once ... Five going twice ... SOLD! This finely crafted violin, an exceptional value, I must say, at $5,000!"*

What "Added Value" Really Means

This story paints a vivid picture of the concept of value — and how to maximize it.

At the beginning of the story the value of the violin was only one dollar. But by the end of the story, that value had jumped an amazing 5,000 percent! All it took to dramatically increase the value of the nearly worthless violin was for one *knowledgeable* person to make *just a few minor adjustments* to the strings ... and then to release the violin's fullest potential by playing it with skill and passion.

The theme of this story — and the theme of the YOU, INC. program — are the same. That is, the value of a product, like the violin ... and the value of a person, like you and me ... can increase 100 times over — even a thousand times over — with just a little fine tuning.

A New Paradigm in Personal Development

YOU, INC. is based on the premise that you are the founder, president, and 100 percent stockholder in your own company — YOU, INCORPORATED.

In other words, YOU, INC. is a whole new way of thinking about yourself and how you relate to the world around you. This book is designed to heighten your awareness and expand your personal paradigm so that you can "discover the CEO within."

In short, in order for us to get the most out of our God-given abilities and talents, we've got to reprogram ourselves to "Think — YOU, INC.!"

Work ON — Not IN — Your Life

Michael Gerber, a world-renowned business consultant, makes the observation that businesses don't fail because of uncontrollable forces, like competition or lack of money or lazy employees.

According to Gerber, the business reflects the person running it ... which is why business owners need to go to work ON their business, not IN their business.

In Gerber's words, *"Your business is nothing more than a distinct reflection of who you are. If your thinking is sloppy, your business will be sloppy. If you are disorganized, then your business will be disorganized. If you are greedy, the people around you will be greedy. So if your business is to change — as it must to be successful — YOU must change."*

In my estimation, Gerber is right on the money. To become truly successful in any endeavor — whether it's business ... or parenting ... or coaching the local Little League baseball team — we have to go to work ON our lives, not IN our lives!

And that, my friends, is what YOU, INC. is all about. What I've set out to do in this book is to focus on the 10 fundamental principles that will empower you to take charge of your business — and your life!

Let me ask you a question: *If you could really and truly improve your value dramatically by understanding and applying the 10 simple principles discussed in this book, would you make them part of your life?*

I certainly hope the answer to this question is YES, because that's the purpose of this book in a nutshell. The 10 principles outlined in this program will empower you to become more valuable in virtually every phase of your life. And as your value increases, you will become more secure in your job ... more productive in your business ... more vital to your family and friends ... in short, happier and more fulfilled in both your professional and personal life.

Why Now More Than Ever

We're living and working in the most exciting age in our world's history — the Information Age — an age of unprecedented change and uncertainty brought about by science fiction-like breakthroughs in technology ... an age of tremendous, almost unimaginable opportunity ... but also an age of massive layoffs, global competition and portable careers.

This is why today, more than ever before in our history, it's *imperative* that we start thinking of ourselves as an independent, self-sufficient business and begin to make our decisions accordingly!

Graduating from the College of Hard Knocks

I'm often asked how I came up with the title for YOU, INC. My response is that YOU, INC. is a new way of thinking and acting. It represents almost 10 years of reading self-help books and biographies ... researching and collecting information ... interviewing successful businessmen and women ... attending countless seminars ... listening to literally hundreds of audios produced by the world's greatest teachers and motivators .. and, last but certainly not least, learning from my own business and personal experiences — both successes and, yes ... failures.

And believe me, I've had my share of failures. I did manage to get a college degree in criminal justice, but it took me five years and two colleges before I finally graduated. Well, I want to tell you, I didn't exactly set the world on fire right away! I didn't want to go into law enforcement, which meant my expensive, hard-earned college degree was basically useless.

At my mother's urging, I signed up to take the test to become an insurance adjustor for Allstate. Much to her amazement, I flunked the exam! Incredible, isn't it? Here I was, a college graduate, and I couldn't even pass a test to qualify for a job paying less than $20,000 a year. Talk about a bust!

I finally landed a job as a boat builder in Sarasota, Florida, earning five dollars and sixty-five cents an hour. A year later I quit to take a job selling cellular phones for commission only.

After selling phones for a year, I decided to open my own business. The good news is, I made a million dollars my first full year in business! The bad news is, it cost me $1.2 million to make it! So here I was, 25 years old, with a wife and a young son ... *and I was $200,000 in debt!*

I won't try to convince you these early failures didn't hurt. I was devastated! But as the old saying goes, "You can't have a rainbow without the rain." These early setbacks rained on my parade alright, but I learned great lessons from them — and in the long run, those early failures changed my life for the better ... forever ... because they forced me to change and grow as a person.

Why the "A" Students Work for the "C" Students

I tell you my story because I want you to know that Burke Hedges is a very average person. I wasn't a child-genius like Bill Gates, who dropped out of Harvard because he was too busy making his first million to attend classes. I was always a C student who had to work hard to make Bs.

But I believed in myself ... I believed that if I got better, my life would get better ... and I believed this country was bursting with opportunity.

In developing YOU, INC., I sought to find the answer to a phenomenon we've all observed: Why is it that the smartest person in your high school algebra class now works the night shift at the post office ... while the kid who flunked algebra now runs a successful insurance agency and owns a home on the beach?

> *"Therefore, get wisdom. And in all thy getting, get understanding."*
>
> *— Proverbs 4:7*

Stop and think about this a second: Why in the world is it that some people from very humble beginnings, like Abraham Lincoln, for example, accomplish so much ... while other people who were born with all the advantages just limp through life?

I was talking with my attorney not long ago about this very phenomenon — that the students who made straight A's in school weren't always the most successful people in life. He smiled and said, *"Burke, we had a saying when I was in law school: 'The A students become law professors. The B students become judges. And the C students make money working for the D students.'"*

Fascinating observation, isn't it?

Well, if brains aren't the key to success, what is? The answer to that question, my friend, is what I'll be sharing with you during the rest of this book.

Intellectual Intelligence vs. Emotional Intelligence

Science has proven that our intellectual intelligence — our IQ, as it's called — is pretty much fixed at birth. No matter how much you study, no matter how motivated you are, you can raise your IQ only a few points.

> *"The door to self improvement only opens from within."*
>
> *— Burke Hedges*

The reality is the A students in law school have real high IQ's. So why is it that so much of the time "the C students make money working for the D students?"

Recent studies show that IQ accounts for only 20 percent of our success in life. The other 80 percent of what we achieve can be attributed to our EMOTIONAL INTELLIGENCE, or EQ.

Sales and management postitions, for example, rely mostly on EQ. Having a happy marriage depends on EQ. Being a good parent ... being a good citizen ... being a good employee ... being a successful entrepreneur ... all depend on EQ.

Now, here's the most exciting news for all of us. EQ, unlike IQ, can be improved at any time during our lives. Which means we can control 80 percent of our achievements. Just as the value of the violin in the opening story was improved dramatically by a simple tuning, so can your fair market value increase dramatically by simply tuning your EQ with the 10 simple principles discussed in this book.

Seek to Understand

My primary goal in the YOU, INC. program is to raise the level of your awareness ... to help you *better understand* what it takes to increase your fair market value. The Bible says it this way: *"Get wisdom. And in all thy getting, get understanding."* "Getting understanding" is really what I want each and every reader to accomplish.

YOU, INC. is designed to help you learn, understand and fine tune the key principles that can sharpen your EQ (and get you that much-deserved promotion) by making your personal skills better, which in turn will make YOU better!

And it only stands to reason that if YOU get better, your job or business will get better.

Doesn't it stand to reason that if you get better, your marriage will get better? ... if you get better, your parenting will get better? ... if you get better, your health will get better? ... if you get better, your relationships will get better?

Doesn't it stand to reason that if you get better, every part of your life will get better? Because when it's all said and done, the only thing you have total control over in your life are the choices YOU make, isn't that true?

Making a Choice to Change

I'd like to tell you a true story about two people who started in exactly the *same place* ... but who ended up in two *very different places* because of the choices each person made.

The story begins one brisk autumn morning when I drove down to Sarasota, Florida, to meet with a book distributor about making our books available in bookstores across the country. Afterward I decided to swing by my old place of work, Dynasty Boat Corporation.

To my surprise, almost 10 years after I left, two of the guys I used to work with were still there! I was delighted to see them again, and we swapped stories about the old days.

As I was about to leave, one of the guys, Bob, popped out of the hull of a 28-foot boat and asked me what I was doing these days. I told him I'd started a couple of businesses and written a couple of books. *"Stay right there,"* I said. *"I think I've got some books in the car. Just a second, and I'll bring you one."*

As I started for the car Bob shouted back, *"Forget the book. If you wanna bring me something, bring me a 12-pack of beer!"*

Everyone broke up laughing, and Bob's co-workers agreed that a cold beer beats a great book every time. I finished my goodbyes to the rest of the crew, and I headed for my car.

As I drove home, I kept thinking about how Bob and I had ended up in two very different places, even though we had started in the same place, sweating side by side in the hull of a boat with a grinder in our hands.

Ten years later Bob was still grunting and sweating for eight bucks an hour. In a good year, with lots of overtime, he may make $18,000. Now, I realize that for many people, $18,000 a year is decent money. But I made a choice when I was working side by side with Bob to improve my YOU, INC. ... I chose to dramatically increase my fair market value so that I could earn a lot more money doing something I loved, instead of settling for $18,000 a year doing something I hated! As a result of my choosing to increase my fair market value by growing as a person, I've often earned $18,000 in a single day! All because I made a choice.

A Book Can Change Your Life

It's obvious why Bob and I had ended up in two very different places. And my visit to Dynasty Boat Corporation reminded me of a simple, yet profound truth:

The door to self improvement only opens from within.

You see, I know firsthand how a book can change someone's life. When I was only 23 years old, my sister-in-law, Susan, gave me a copy of Og Mandino's, *The Greatest Salesman in the World.* Instead of tossing that book in a corner and grabbing a beer, I read it. I made a conscious choice to open the door to self improvement! I made a conscious choice to make myself better by FINDING REASONS TO increase my value, instead of FINDING REASONS NOT TO.

And that, my friend, has made a world of difference in my life.

The Greatest Salesman in the World was the first step to expanding my horizons from a boat hull to the ocean of opportunity available in America today.

Now, some of you may still be wondering if the principles in YOU, INC. can really work for *average* people.

Not the super talented.

Not the super rich.

Not the super beautiful.

But just the average Joe and Jane.

When it's all said and done, what every single person reading this book wants to know is CAN THESE PRINCIPLES WORK FOR ME?

Added Value Equals Added Income

The best way to answer that question is for you to hear a story about an average person with an average job. His name is Walter. And his job is driving a cab in New York City. Now, is that average enough for you? Well, listen to what happened to Walter the Cab Driver when he "discovered the CEO within" by thinking and acting like YOU, INC. — instead of thinking and acting like just another cab driver in a city full of cab drivers.

I heard about the story of Walter the Cab Driver, by the way, from Harvey McKay, author of *Swim with the Sharks Without Being Eaten Alive!* When I first heard McKay's account of Walter, I was absolutely blown away, because his story proves that the concept of YOU, INC. is alive and well, right in the driver's seat of a cab cruising around the streets of Manhattan.

Let me preface this story by reminding you that if you travel at all, especially in big cities like New York, you probably don't have much good to say about the typical cab ride.

A Typical Cab Ride

The typical cab ride for me goes something like this: The driver is a burly guy with a two-day-old beard. The cab looks like it hasn't been washed since it rolled off the assembly line five years earlier.

The inside smells like an ashtray ... and, more often than not, the driver has a lit cigarette dangling from his lips as he throws your bags into a dirty trunk.

And then the fun really begins. The driver stops traffic with a wave of his hand and pulls across three lanes, screaming at the drivers who have the nerve to honk at him. He swerves in and out of traffic ... tailgates every chance he gets ... never uses his turn signal ... and mutters profanities under his breath as he avoids one life-threatening accident after another.

> *"Why is it, then, that so many people ... who could BE so much more ... and who could HAVE so much more ... are choosing to settle for less? "*
>
> — *Burke Hedges*

Does that cab ride sound familiar? Sadly, this is about the norm when it comes to cab rides. When I jump into the backseat of a cab, let's just say I don't have high expectations for enjoying the trip. In fact, my primary goal is to get where I'm going in one piece.

Now I ask you, where is it written that a cab ride is an experience to be *endured*, rather than *enjoyed*? Wouldn't you reward a cab driver who increased his fair market value by going out of his way to make your experience a delightful adventure? I certainly would! Here's McKay's version of his delightful experience with Walter the Cab Driver:

YOU, INC. in Action

McKay was checking out of a Manhattan hotel heading for La Guardia Airport when he jumped into the back of Walter's cab. The cab, by the way, looked like just about every other cab in New York — except for the fact the cab was dent free and freshly washed and waxed. So McKay was sitting in a cab parked in front of a mid-Manhattan hotel waiting for yet another cab ride to the airport when Walter hands him a sheet of paper with the following message printed on it:

"Hi, my name is Walter, and I'm your driver. Rest assured that I will get you to your destination comfortably, safely and on time. If there is anything I can do to make your trip more enjoyable, please let me know, and I'll happily oblige."

Of course, McKay was surprised, to say the least. He thought to himself that he's ridden in thousands of cabs ... thousands of times ... with thousands of different drivers, and this was the first time a driver ever handed him a written mission statement!

Then Walter politely turned to McKay, held up two daily newspapers and asked, *"Would you prefer today's New York Times or the Post?"*

A suspicious McKay asked, *"How much?"* Walter replied, *"Complimentary, sir."* Now, McKay was starting to become pretty impressed with Walter the Cab Driver, and he took a moment to survey the cab's interior more closely.

McKay noticed that the cab was spotless. There was no smell of stale tobacco smoke in Walter's cab — just an understated scent of carpet shampoo and light air freshener. McKay noticed that Walter was clean shaven. He was wearing a starched white shirt, a necktie and a classic blue blazer. McKay was becoming more and more impressed by the minute.

> *"It's not the mountains we conquer, but ourselves."*
>
> *— Sir Edmund Hillary*

"Excuse me, sir," Walter said politely. *"I have several radio stations for your listening enjoyment. Would you prefer popular music, rock, or classical? Or, if you prefer, I have a wide assortment of CD's."*

By this time McKay was in a mild state of shock. Here he was, sitting in a cab in New York City, receiving the same first-class, cordial service as he received in the five-star hotel he just checked out of. Walter's cab was like having room service on wheels.

"Excuse me for interrupting, sir," Walter said gently. *"But I was wondering if you'd be interested in a healthy snack?"* Then Walter held up a decorated fruit basket filled to the brim with ripe red apples ... oranges ... bananas ... and assorted low-fat cheeses, crackers and cookies.

McKay goes on and on about all the little amenities that Walter offered him during his 30-minute ride to the airport. McKay ends the story by saying he so enjoyed the experience that he gave Walter a sizable tip. In fact, in talking to Walter, McKay learned that he wasn't the only person who thought Walter was deserving of a big tip. According to McKay, Walter earns an extra $12 to $14 THOUSAND PER YEAR IN TIPS!

Putting the 10 Principles into Practice

When you think about it, what's amazing isn't that Walter went to all these lengths to make sure his fares enjoyed their rides. What's amazing is that Walter's extra service was so *rare* that people are amazed by it — even frequent travelers like Harvey McKay! And to think all Walter did was to realize he was founder, president and 100 precent stockholder in Walter, Inc. ... and to act accordingly.

Walter increased the value of a low-paying, low-status job by 33 to 50 percent, just by instinctively understanding ... fine tuning ... and then applying the simple principles I'll be sharing with you in the coming pages.

For example, *he took responsibility* for his success ... *he dreamed and planned* about a better, more productive, more profitable way to deliver his services ... *he believed* he could introduce services that would increase his value ... *he acted on his dreams* by putting his ideas into practice, instead of just talking about them ... *he elevated his attitude,* and in the process, elevated the attitude of everyone who entered his cab ... *he developed productive habits* that became as natural to him as breathing ... *he prepared to achieve* more in his life through observation ... research ... and empathy .... And finally, *he made the choice to change* from a run-of-the-mill cab driver to a cab-driver *extraordinaire!*

The Power of Choice

I love this story because it's a perfect example of how a person can choose excellence over mediocrity — and profit in the process!

New York City is full of mediocre cab drivers ... earning a mediocre income ... leading mediocre lives. Then along comes Walter to remind us that average people in average jobs don't have to settle for mediocrity.

We can choose to grow.

We can choose to understand.

We can choose to get better.

We can choose to change.

And in so doing, we are choosing to transform our lives from ordinary ... to *extra-ordinary.*

You and I both know that every cab driver could make the kinds of choices that Walter made. I know beyond a shadow of a doubt that every doorman ... every police officer ... every stockbroker ... every retiree ... every man and every woman in every city of the world ... could make the kinds of choices that Walter made.

Why is it, then, that so many people who could BE so much more ... and who could HAVE so much more ... are choosing to settle for less? ... Why is it that so many people are just willing to go through the motions? ... to look at the cup of life as if it were half empty, instead of half full? ... and to drive through life with their foot on the brake?

The answer to those questions, I've got to believe, isn't that people are stupid. Or disadvantaged. Or without talent. The answer, I think, is that far too many people lack wisdom and understanding about how to increase their value and improve their lives.

I've got to believe that if more people understood — I mean, really and truly *understood*— how to increase their value ... if more people really and truly *understood* the principles that lead to excellence and what can happen to their lives when they apply these time-tested principles of success ... that the world would undergo a magical transformation.

YOU, INC. Is Based on Sound Business Principles

At first glance, it may seem like the 10 principles you're going to hear about are unrelated to the corporate world. On the contrary, every successful company embodies all of these principles.

For example, doesn't every successful business start with a dream? Isn't the word "Attitude" the same thing as a company's image or brand name? Don't companies prepare themselves for success by investing in research and development ... and by training their employees? Don't companies respond to change with new products and marketing strategies?

I can't emphasize enough that this program is based on fundamental, universal truths that apply equally to every enterprise, whether it's an individual ... or a Fortune 500 company. In short, the principles in YOU, INC. will empower you to go to work ON your life, not IN your life!

Conquering Ourselves

Sir Edmund Hillary, the first man to climb to the top of Mt. Everest, understood as much as anyone the importance of self-improvement. He said, and I quote: *"It's not the mountains we conquer, but ourselves."*

No one ever said that conquering the peaks of tall mountains was easy. Likewise, no one ever said that conquering yourself through personal growth was going to be easy, either. But I will say this: No matter what the struggle ... no matter what the sacrifice ... over a lifetime, it's worth it to make the effort to conquer yourself.

Always remember: The price you will pay for choosing to live a life of mediocrity is much higher than the price you will pay to enjoy success ... prosperity ... and happiness.

During the course of this book, I will share invaluable information with you — information that has the power to change your life dramatically!

What you choose to do with this information is up to you. However, I guarantee you this: If you will commit to fully understanding these principles ... and then commit to making them a part of your everyday life, your value — like the value of the violin in the opening story — will SKYROCKET!

• • •

SECTION 2

. . .

10 Simple Principles to Dramatically Increase Your Fair Market Value

An army of principles will penetrate where an army of soldiers will not ... and it will conquer!

> — Thomas Paine
> from *Common Sense*

PRINCIPLE 1:
Take Responsibility

*You cannot escape the responsibility
of tomorrow by evading it today.*
— Abraham Lincoln

I'm sitting here looking at two very different articles in the same edition of my local newspaper. See if you can tell which article warms my heart ... and which one makes my blood boil!

The first article is by a columnist for the *Tampa Tribune* who decided not to make anymore New Year's resolutions because they all end up broken anyway.

Her reasoning goes like this: You make a bunch of promises to yourself, like you resolve to quit smoking. Then you break those promises, which makes you feel guilty. Since feeling guilty makes you feel lousy, what's the point of making resolutions?

Her solution? Here are her exact words: *"There's a simple solution to avoid all this — to feel good about yourself while keeping guilt at bay. Don't make resolutions."*

Now, this is the same middle-aged columnist who is always whining about the fact she can't quit smoking. This is the same columnist who looks to be *at least 40 pounds overweight.*

Founding Father of the Fitness Movement

The other article is about a man named Ken Cooper. Here's what the newspaper had to say about Ken Cooper's amazing life.

When Cooper was 29 years old, he accepted an invitation to go water skiing. A former hot-shot athlete in high school, Cooper thought he could pick up where he left off 10 years before.

Only one problem. For 10 years he'd been in college and medical school. He hadn't made time in his busy schedule to work out or eat right, and his ideal weight of 165 had ballooned to more than 200 pounds.

Despite being woefully out of shape, Cooper attacked the slalom course just as he used to do in high school. But his body, flabby and weak from inactivity, gave up on him. He barely made it back to the beach ... *and then collapsed!*

> *"Our charge on earth is to exercise our gifts and talents to the maximum — and to care for all the assets God has given us, including our bodies."*
>
> — Dr. Ken Cooper

Nausea swept over him. His heart was hammering at 250 beats per minute! In Cooper's words, "*I was terrified. I thought I was going to die.*"

That episode was a turning point in Cooper's life. He began running ... watching his diet. Six months later he had dropped 30 pounds and his blood pressure returned to normal. Thirty years after that incident, Cooper still weighs 165 pounds and is in better shape than most men half his age!

You see, Ken Cooper became Dr. Ken Cooper, the man who coined the word "aerobics" and who helped launch the fitness revolution in the early 1960s. He has authored numerous books on fitness and established the Cooper Center for Aerobics Research in Dallas. Cooper's philosophy can be summed up in this short paragraph from his latest book, *It's Better to Believe.*

"*Our charge on this earth is to exercise our gifts and talents to the maximum — and to care for all the assets God has given us, including our bodies.*"

Taking Responsibility vs. Taking the Easy Way Out

Now I ask you, which of these two individuals would you rather be? Active and fit in your fifties, like Dr. Ken Cooper ... or inactive and overweight, like the cigarette-addicted columnist?

I'm telling you about these two people because they have opposite approaches to the concept of responsibility. One person took responsibility for his health ... while the other person took the easy way out by making excuses for NOT taking responsibility for her health.

I know firsthand what it means to take responsibility for my health. You see, for about 10 years I smoked cigarettes. And I've battled a weight problem all my life. In fact, I weighed more than 230 pounds at one point, even though I'm only about five feet ten inches tall.

I swear, when I was in my mid-twenties I looked like the rotund actor who played Cannon on TV. The truth is, I looked like a cannonball! Today, I'm proud to say, I'm smoke free and I've kept my weight under control.

Just imagine where I would be if I had taken the columnist's position. I'd still be making lame excuses instead of making needed changes in my life. I'd still be smoking cigarettes ... and I'd still look like the Pillsbury Doughboy. But I had sense enough to do what Dr. Ken Cooper did — I TOOK RESPONSIBILITY FOR MY LIFE!

I didn't make excuses. I didn't blame McDonald's for making high-fat burgers and fries; I didn't blame Phillip Morris for seducing me into smoking cigarettes with their slick ads. No way! I did what any *responsible* person would do — I made a commitment to improve my health by quitting smoking and losing weight. And believe me, I've never felt better in my life!

The Real Meaning of Responsibility

Let's take a moment to talk about responsibility — what it is and why it's so important in our lives. The dictionary defines responsibility as *"readily assuming obligations or duties."*

That pretty much says it all. But an even better definition is President Harry Truman's oft-quoted statement: THE BUCK STOPS HERE!

Truman was referring, of course, to the pastime of our country's elected politicians, who are always blaming someone else ... always "passing the buck." Well, "Give 'em Hell Harry," as he was called, wasn't afraid to step up to the plate. He knew that each and every person was responsible for who they are and what they become ... and that included himself.

Look, I understand the position the columnist took — but that doesn't mean I have to agree with it. Like I said, she's taking the easy way out. She turned her back on responsibility because it's a lot easier to *avoid* responsibility than to *accept* responsibility. She turned her back on responsibility because it's a lot easier to pass the buck than to stand up and proclaim: THE BUCK STOPS HERE!

"It's Not My Fault, Daddy!"

I have four wonderful children under the age of 10, three boys and a girl. What's most amazing about my kids is they all have the same answer when one of them gets in trouble: IT'S NOT MY FAULT, DADDY! You see, with four active kids in the house, things go wrong from time to time — toys get left out in the rain ... lunches get left behind on the kitchen counter ... tomorrow's homework gets left in the locker at school. You get the idea!

When my wife Debbie and I ask any of the kids what went wrong, they usually answer, "IT'S NOT MY FAULT." Now, I can understand the answer "IT'S NOT MY FAULT" from a child. I don't condone that answer, mind you ... but I understand it.

If you were anything like me when I was a kid, you tried to "fib" your way out of accepting responsibility by blaming the wind ... or a bird ... or a brother — anybody but yourself! Again, that's not to say it's acceptable when a youngster avoids responsibility — but it is understandable.

There comes a time in every person's life, however, when IT'S NOT MY FAULT is no longer acceptable. There's a time in every person's life when they must stand up and say, THE BUCK STOPS HERE.

What saddens me about this great country of ours is that so many of our citizens are frozen in a permanent state of arrested development! Somewhere along the way we've evolved from a nation of people with a CAN DO attitude ... to a nation of people with a IT'S-NOT-MY-FAULT approach to life. In short, too many of us spend our time *avoiding responsibility* by blaming others rather than *accepting responsibility* by tackling our challenges head on.

Where Were the Parents?

Let's take a moment to talk about some all-too-common situations where people go out of their way to avoid their responsibilities. For example, does it bother you when you hear about 13-year-old kids getting arrested at 3:30 in the morning for stealing a car? The first thing I think of is, "Where were the parents?" What kind of parent would allow a 13-year-old kid to run around at 3:30 in the morning? An irresponsible parent, that's what kind!

So, what do these irresponsible parents do? They blame the school system.

They blame the juvenile justice system.

They blame the neighborhood.

They blame their kid's friends.

They even go so far as to blame the police for doing their jobs!

They blame everyone but the persons who are most at blame — namely, themselves!

What about people who get drunk at the local tavern ... and then run a red light while driving home, totaling their car and injuring an innocent person in the process? So what do these drunks do? ... They sue the tavern owner for serving them too much booze!

And what about the people who smoke two packs of cigarettes a day for 35 years and then sue the tobacco companies when they get lung cancer? How absurd is this?

Profiting from Irresponsibility

If that's not bad enough, many of these irresponsible people are actually winning these ridiculous lawsuits! It's sad! It's not enough we've got people who are shirking responsibility — they're profiting from it! What's going on here? Has the world gone mad?

The most amazing story I've ever heard about irresponsible people trying to profit from their negligence happened in Camden, New Jersey. An 18-year-old was jailed for murdering a shopkeeper. While awaiting trial on the fifth floor of the Camden County Jail, the teen-ager and four of his convict friends decided to escape. They cut a hole in one of the outside windows and were lowering themselves down a rope made from tied-up bedsheets.

The teen-ager lost his balance during the attempted jail-break and fell to his death. So what did his parents do? You guessed it ... they sued the city on the grounds the jail officials failed to maintain, in their words, *"a reasonably safe facility."*

Is it just me, or have these people lost their minds? Rather than suing the city for their child's accidental death, they should be agonizing over the murder their son committed and examining the way they raised him. Do you think a responsible parent ... or a responsible citizen ... would avoid their responsibility and try to pin the blame on someone else? NOT A CHANCE!

Here's a shocking statistic. Do you know how many civil lawsuits are filed in this country every year? The answer will astound you — 20 MILLION ... 20 MILLION A YEAR! I've got to believe that a great deal of those lawsuits are filed by people looking to blame someone else for their irresponsible, careless actions, like cigarette smokers who come down with lung cancer and then sue the tobacco company. Pretty pathetic, isn't it?

Look, the simple fact is you can't make YOU better — or your job better ... or your health better ... or your finances better ... or your relationships better — by blaming everything on somebody else. The way to make YOU, INC. better isn't to blame THEY, INC. ... whether THEY are the police ... or the politicians ... or the rich people ... or the conservatives or the liberals ... or whoever! The way to make YOU, INC. better is for you to take total responsibility for your life.

When YOU Do It, You Know It Gets Done

For example, some friends of mine got upset because there's too much trash in their neighborhood. So they organized the neighbors to write letters blaming the city for not picking up the litter. Do you really think that made the trash go away? Of course not. In fact, the last I heard, their neighborhood was still covered with litter.

Instead of organizing a letter-writing campaign, what if my friends had organized a litter pick-up patrol? Accepting responsibility by PICKING UP THE LITTER would clean up the neighborhood FOR CERTAIN, wouldn't it? When it's all said and done, YOU, INC. is responsible for cleaning up your neighborhood, not the city. YOU, INC. is responsible for cleaning up YOUR LIFE ... not someone else! The same could be said for every facet of our lives.

The Rewards of Responsibility

If everyone took responsibility for their diet and exercise, one third of Americans overweight wouldn't be out of shape, would they?

If everyone took responsibility for increasing their income and saving toward their retirement, we wouldn't have to rely on social security to make ends meet, would we?

If everyone took responsibility to help their kids with their homework, we wouldn't have high school graduates who can't read and write, would we?

My position on personal responsibility is like the car ad I see from time to time on TV, where the announcer says, *"There are two kinds of people on the road of life. Passengers and drivers!"*

People who take responsibility are the drivers of the world; people who don't are the passengers. The drivers are in control of their lives ... the drivers are calling the shots ... the drivers are making the decisons on which way to turn and how fast to go ... the drivers are having fun and living with passion ... the drivers are enjoying the fruits of taking responsibility.

> *"There are two kinds of people on the road of life. Passengers and drivers!"*
>
> — *TV commercial for Volkswagen*

The passengers, on the other hand, are just along for the ride. Passengers are just spectators, watching the world go by instead of choosing to actively participate. Passengers are "backseat" drivers who are more comfortable second-guessing the drivers and telling them where they *should have turned*, instead of getting behind the wheel themselves.

Can you see why drivers of the world are more fulfilled? ... Happier? ... More independent? ... More purposeful? ... More confident? ... Like people who seek and accept responsibility, drivers *make things happen*, instead of looking out the window and *watching things happen.*

Here's the bottom line: YOU, and only you — not your mom and dad ... not Uncle Sam ... not your employer ... not THEY, INC. — are responsible for your life. Accepting responsibility for your life is what separates the adults from the children ... the men from the boys ... the achievers from the wanna be's ... the winners from the losers.

Think of it this way: If you smoke cigarettes, did anyone put a gun to your head and force you to start? Can anyone quit smoking for you? Can anyone lose weight for you? Can anyone go to college for you? ... Learn a trade for you? ... Read this book for you? Of course not! Only you can!

When it's all said and done, YOU are responsible for the success or failure ... improvement or stagnation of YOU, INC.! You are responsible for your own actions ... you are responsible for creating your own dreams and setting your own goals ... you are responsible for believing in yourself ... for improving your attitude ... for replacing bad habits with good ones ... for preparing for success ... for controlling your emotions ... for managing your time, and so on.

Taking Responsibility for YOU, INC.

Look at it this way: Would you want to work for a company that didn't take responsibility for the quality of its products? ... or a company that shipped half its orders to the wrong addresses? Would you want to work for a president of a company who forgot to show up at board meetings? Would you want to work for a profitable company that failed to pay you? Of course not! That kind of behavior is irresponsible.

Then how do you think people would feel about your company — YOU, INC. — if you avoided responsibility?

How do you think people would feel about YOU, INC. if you always showed up late to important meetings?

How do you think people would feel about YOU, INC. if you wrote checks that bounced?

How do you think people would feel about YOU, INC. if you were always negative and complaining at work?

Do you think your value in their eyes would increase ... or decrease ... if you failed to meet your responsibilities?

The long and short of it is the only person who can add value to your life is YOU ... AND YOU KNOW IT! Look, I know for a fact that things aren't going very well right now for lots and lots of Americans. Maybe YOU are one of those people.

Don't Play the Blame Game

Maybe YOU are one of those people who is up to your eyeballs in debt, about to lose your home or car — so you're blaming the economy!

Maybe YOU are one of those people who is overworked and underpaid ... so you're blaming your boss!

Maybe YOU are one of those people who has been laid off ... so you're blaming your old company.

If this sounds all too familiar, maybe YOU are falling into the "blaming trap." Justifying your failures by blaming someone else may add conversation to your pity party, but it won't change anything. When it's all said and done, the only one who can change your life is you ... and all the blaming in the world won't ever change that fact!

From Outhouse to Penthouse

Perhaps we can best illustrate the importance of taking responsibility by sharing a story about a man named Tim who turned his life around 180 degrees by choosing to take responsibility.

Tim was raised in a middle-class family with five brothers and sisters. At age 11, fate dealt him a terrible blow — his father was killed in an automobile accident. After struggling through high school and college, Tim got caught up in a fast, hard-partying crowd. Foolishly, he started selling cocaine, and in 1979 he was arrested and sentenced to eight years in prison.

Getting Better Instead of Bitter

Instead of sinking into bitterness and blaming "society" while he was in jail, Tim went to work on himself. He came to the realization that he had messed up, and if he were ever going to make anything of his life, it was up to him.

Many years later Tim said, *"I had a lot of anger during that time in my life, but I realized I had to direct the anger at me, not someone else. I finally took the blame for this whole situation I put myself in."*

He spent his time improving himself by reading books and writing. A naturally funny guy, Tim started organizing prison talent shows, acting as the master of ceremonies, where he tried out new jokes and comedy bits. Upon his release from prison, Tim went to work in an advertising agency and perfected his comedy act at local clubs in the evenings.

Eventually his performance caught the attention of several Disney executives, who offered him a starring role in a TV comedy series. Even though Tim was desperate to break into the big time, he turned down Disney's first programming idea. After turning down two more suggestions from the Disney people, Tim decided to take responsibility for the direction of his career. So he came up with his own idea for a show — a series about the host of a TV handyman show.

By now you have probably guessed that Tim's full name is Tim Allen, star of ABC's *Home Improvement*! In 1994, only 10 years after he was released from federal prison, Tim went on to score a rare triple play: He was starring in the number-one TV show. His first movie, *The Santa Clause*, became the surprise hit of the Christmas season. And his joke-filled autobiography reached number one on the *New York Times* best seller list! What a comeback!

Added Value Equals Added Income

Now, let me ask you a question. Do you really think Tim Allen would have become a superstar if he had NOT accepted responsibility for his mistakes? We both know the answer to that, don't we?

Think about this: What was Tim Allen's *value* to his friends ... to his family ... to his wife .... and to society at large while he was still in prison? I think it's fair to say, very little. But can you see how he dramatically *increased his value* to everyone around him by understanding and living just one of the simple principles in this program — the principle of taking responsibility?

This is why it's crucial to understand the power behind Principle One: *Take Responsibility*. The application of this one principle alone can add enormous value to YOU, INC.! How much do you think Tim Allen earned for starring in his first movie? About $10 million, plus a percentage of the gross profits! Not bad for an ex-con!

> *"Liberty means responsibility. That's why most men dread it."*
>
> — George Bernard Shaw

Now can you see how accepting responsibility for who you are and what you become can dramatically increase your value to your profession ... your family ... and your friends? It's the difference between an ordinary life ... and an EXTRA-ORDINARY LIFE!

My blood boils when I hear about influential people, like the overweight smoking newspaper columnist, who advocate *avoiding responsibility* rather than accepting responsibility. That's why I go through the roof when I hear stories about "dead-beat dads" who father children and then walk away from their responsibility to them. Not only do their actions hurt other people, they hurt themselves!

Irresponsibility Is a Double-Edged Sword

That's the whole point about avoiding responsibility — it's a double-edged sword. It affects you, as well as others! For example, I feel very sorry for people who abandon their children to satisfy their own pleasures. Not only is it devastating for the children, but also the neglectful parent misses out on perhaps the single greatest joy that life has to offer — the experience of loving a child and guiding that child from birth into adulthood!

Parents who park their children in front of a TV for five, six hours at a time might think they are avoiding the hassles of dealing with their children ... but what these parents don't realize is THEY are the ones missing out.

You see, irresponsible parents miss out on the opportunity to influence their children's future ... Irresponsible parents miss out on the opportunity to guide their children into adulthood ... Irresponsible parents miss out on the opportunity to nurture a lifelong closeness with their children.

> *"I am only one,*
> *but still I am one;*
> *I cannot do everything,*
> *but still I can*
> *do something;*
> *I will NOT refuse*
> *to do the something*
> *I can do."*
>
> — *Helen Keller*

Responsibility Is a Joy, Not a Job

The great Irish playwright George Bernard Shaw made this observation about responsibility: *"Liberty means responsibility. That's why most men dread it."* That's true, especially in this day and age. What Shaw neglected to mention were the benefits of taking responsibility! Rather than dreading responsibility, people should seek it out because no one can ever be truly fulfilled until they eagerly seek out and accept responsibility.

Just think about the experiences that have given you the deepest sense of satisfaction. Didn't you feel good about yourself when you took responsibility and lost 15 pounds? ...

Didn't you feel good about yourself when you took responsibility and helped a friend who was down and out? ...

Didn't you feel good about yourself when you took responsibility and passed that tough examination you'd been dreading?

Didn't you feel good about yourself when you took responsibility and graduated from high school or college ... or saved the money to buy your first home ... or stuck to your New Year's resolutions? Of course you did! Those accomplishments gave you a deep sense of satisfaction and made you feel fulfilled, worthwhile and valuable.

Let me ask you a question — what gives you a deeper sense of satisfaction ... putting things up ... or putting things off? Driving the car ... or riding in the car? Achieving success by accepting responsibility for YOU, INC. ... or accepting mediocrity and blaming it on THEY, INC.? I think anyone who has ever accepted responsibility and seen it through to the end would know, without a shadow of a doubt, which of these choices leads to a greater sense of satisfaction.

Embracing Responsibility

The point is this: Taking responsibility is NOT something we should seek to avoid — it's something we must embrace if we want to experience all of the great rewards that life has to offer!

> *"Life isn't about finding yourself. Life is about creating yourself."*
>
> *— Mary McCarthy*

A perfect example is when I accepted the responsibility to quit smoking. I'll guarantee you, the genuine, long-term satisfaction I received from quitting smoking was far greater than the short-term satisfaction I ever got from lighting up a cigarette! And that's just one small example that illustrates the enormous benefits of taking responsibility.

The famous American novelist Mary McCarthy once said that *"Life isn't about finding yourself. Life is about creating yourself."*

What a message! You certainly don't have control over the gift of life, no one would argue with that. But what about the rest of your life — the life you choose to *create* for yourself starting right this very moment? The challenge is to *create yourself* by making an unconditional commitment to take responsibility for every aspect of your life. All you have to do is say, *"Beginning today, I assume total responsibility for who I am and what I become."*

Congratulations! You just made a vow that has the power to make you more valuable than you ever dreamed.

Now let's take some time to examine and understand those dreams in the next chapter, *Principle Two: Dare to Dream!*

• • •

PRINCIPLE 2: _____

Dare to Dream

> *The future belongs to those who believe*
> *in the beauty of their dreams.*
> — Eleanor Roosevelt

I t's a shame that all too often we associate the word "dreams" with unrealistic expectations. We've been conditioned to think of dreams as unattainable, calling them "pipe dreams" and "day dreams."

On the contrary, dreams don't have to be *unreal*. Dreams are the mental pictures that inspire virtually every *real* human endeavor, from the ancient Egyptians' dreams of building the Great Pyramids ... to *your dream* of starting a family or building a new home.

In Napoleon Hill's immortal words, *"All achievement and all earthly riches have their beginnings in an idea or a dream."* Does that definition sound like it's describing something *unreal*? Not at all!

Dreams contain nearly limitless power to lift us up in a world that sometimes seems determined to hold us down.

Dreams have the power to pull us forward in the face of adversity.

Dreams have the power to sharpen our focus and fill our lives with energy and passion.

Dreams have the power to renew our strength and shield us from criticism and negative thinking.

But most of all, dreams have the power to remind us that the biggest accomplishments always start with the biggest dreams. To use another classic quote from Napoleon Hill: *"Anything the mind can conceive ... and the heart can believe ... you can achieve."*

Dreaming His Way to the Top

Here's a story about a man named Lou who personified Hill's

observation that if you can conceive it ... and believe it ... you can achieve it!

When Lou was in his mid-twenties, he showed up to work one morning only to be greeted by the news that every employee fears — he'd been fired! A proud, determined man, Lou was deeply hurt by his dismissal. He hung around the house for several days, feeling sorry for himself and blaming the world for his misfortune.

> *"All achievement and all earthly riches have their beginnings in an idea or a dream."*
>
> — Napoleon Hill

But Lou understood that feeling sorry for himself was getting him nowhere fast! So one day shortly after his firing, Lou decided to turn his negative experience into a positive one by using the time between jobs as an opportunity to plan the rest of his life.

Lou started by sitting alone in a quiet room and *dreaming* about all of the things he'd like to accomplish in his life. Then he took out a piece of paper and began jotting his dreams down as fast as he could.

When Lou finished, he had a list of 107 dreams. Some involved adventure, like sky diving. Some were lofty, like accepting a dinner invitation to the White House. Some involved his family, like seeing all four of his children graduate from college. And some were so ambitious they were almost impossible for Lou to reach.

Become a Possibility Thinker

But while Lou was making his dream list, he didn't worry about being overly realistic. He didn't want to think about all the things he could NOT do. He didn't want to dwell on limitations. He wanted to concentrate on the things he *could* do. He wanted to concentrate on *possibility thinking*, not pessimistic thinking. He made it a point to dream again!

Because Lou *DARED TO DREAM*, he not only turned his life around ... he became one of the most successful people in the history of his chosen profession. You see, one of Lou's dreams was to become head coach of the Notre Dame football team. Another was to coach his team to a national championship.

Amazingly, Lou — whose full name is Lou Holtz — achieved both! In 1988, Lou Holtz coached his undefeated Notre Dame football team to a national championship!

Lou accomplished not only those two dreams ... but 93 others from his original list of 107 dreams. Just think, Lou accomplished almost *90 percent* of his dreams. Lou's accomplishments are living proof that dreaming has the awesome power to transform people's lives!

The Magical Power of Dreaming

The Lou Holtz story emphasizes the magical power of dreaming. Everywhere I look around this great country of ours, I see overwhelming evidence of the real power of dreaming ... starting with the most cherished possession of every American, our freedom!

Can you imagine where you and I would be if our founding fathers had NOT dared to dream? *We'd still be a colony of England!* Without a dream, America, the Land of the Free, would still be the land of the world's largest plantation!

But because the signers of the Declaration of Independence DARED TO DREAM more than 200 years ago, America is today the international model for democracy and the leader of the free world. That's what I mean, my friend, when I say there's power in dreaming big dreams!

How to Turn Your Dreams into Reality

What I'd like to do now is talk about a proven method for turning your dreams into reality. During the rest of this chapter you will learn about the importance of dreams and how to turn those dreams into a vision for your future. You'll learn how to write a mission statement for YOU, INC. And last but not least, you'll learn how to translate your dreams into long-term and short-term goals!

Let's get started by discussing the three simple stages necessary to start turning your dreams ... into your destiny.

Stage one is **THINK** your dream.

Stage two is **VISUALIZE** your dream.

And stage three is **PLAN** your dream.

To better understand how these stages work, let's look at how a real estate developer might go about turning his dreams into reality.

First, the developer would start at stage one by *thinking about his dream.* He would visit a tract of undeveloped land, and he'd begin to think about what it would take to turn raw acreage into a bustling subdivision of new homes.

In the second stage he would begin to *visualize his dream in his mind's eye*, imagining where the streets and houses and parks might be.

Finally, if he were convinced the project was feasible, he would graduate to the third stage and start *planning his dream* by drawing up a site plan and setting project goals. The better a developer is at each of these stages, the better his final product.

The same can be said for YOU, INC. The better you are at *thinking ... visualizing ...* and *planning* your dreams, the better your chances of making those dreams come true.

Every successful company goes through these same stages. Every Fortune 500 company started with a big dream ... shaped that dream into a compelling vision ... and then went about the business of realizing that vision by working toward short-term and long-term goals.

The Difference Between a Dream and a Fantasy

Before we discuss each of these three stages in more detail, let's define the word DREAM and talk about how a dream is different from a concept that is so often confused with dreams, namely, a fantasy.

Let's begin by describing what a dream is NOT! A dream is NOT a fantasy. A fantasy can be defined as *"unattainable, child-like imaginings."*

When you were a child, you may have fantasized that you were Superman or Wonder Woman. It didn't take long for you to outgrow that fantasy, did it? Even at a young age, we understood that flying like Superman was "unattainable."

Even though fantasies are "child-like imaginings," most adults "escape reality" from time to time by slipping off into fantasies. A perfect example of an adult fantasy is the lottery. In fact, the Florida lottery has one game called "Fantasy 500." The name tells you exactly what it is — yet, amazingly, adults who are old enough to know better still throw away their hard-earned money on lottery tickets.

> *"A dream is a blueprint for your ultimate achievements."*
>
> *— Napoleon Hill*

The truth is, you *literally* have a better chance of getting hit by lightning than winning the lottery! It's sad that so many smart, intelligent Americans suppress their dreams ... yet continue to cling to a childish fantasy of winning the lottery!

Unlike a fantasy, dreams can come true! A great definition of a dream is this one: *A dream is a blueprint for your ultimate achievements.* In other words, when you dream, your emotions tell your imagination to draw up a mental picture of a place you'd like to be in your life. The difference between a dream and a fantasy is that dreams are attainable. Dreams can be fantastic and far out, like inventing the electric lightbulb or putting a man on the moon. But they have to be concrete and attainable, otherwise, they're fantasies!

That's why I say there's a world of difference between *fantasizing and dreaming!* Years ago when I was building boats during those hot Florida summers, I'd come home after work and stand in a cold shower, scrubbing the fiberglass out of my forearms with a stiff scrubbing brush.

I remember sitting on the beat-up couch in our one-bedroom apartment DREAMING about the day I'd live in a big, beautiful home surrounded by lots of children ...

I'd dream about driving a new luxury car instead of a beat-up old Datsun ...

I'd dream about being debt free and having cash in the bank ...

I'd dream about owning my own business and controlling my own future. You see, while my friends at work were *fantasizing* about winning the lottery, I was dreaming ... visualizing ... and planning a *realistic* way to accomplish those dreams.

Well, because I *dared to dream* 10 years ago, today those dreams have become a reality! Now, does that mean my quest is over ... does that mean I should quit dreaming? Not at all. Dreaming is an on going process ... a journey, not a destination. That's why today I have a whole new set of dreams. God willing, in 10 years I'll be living most of those dreams ... while thinking up new dreams for the next 10 years!

Stage One: Think Your Dream

Let's return to our discussion of the three stages of dreaming and talk some more about each stage, starting with stage one, THINK YOUR DREAM. When you *think your dream*, it means you do what Lou Holtz did when he was a young man just starting out — you've got to sit down and brainstorm about all the things you'd like to achieve in your life — and then write them down.

Do you think Lou Holtz would remember all 107 dreams if he had NOT written them down? Not a chance. So let your imagination go ... and then write down a laundry list of those dreams.

If you get "writer's block" trying to think of dreams, you might try asking WHAT IF questions. WHAT IF questions get your imagination clicking again. Ask yourself, "*What if* I could have any job in the world ... what would it be? *What if* money and time weren't a problem ... what would I do with the rest of my life?" Answers to *what if* questions like these can get your dreams flowing faster and stronger than ever!

Stage Two: Visualize Your Dream

Stage two in turning your dreams into reality is to VISUALIZE YOUR DREAM. When you *visualize*, you start with a vague idea of what it is you want, and then you sharpen the focus until the picture becomes clear and sharp in your mind. It's sort of like watching a Polaroid picture develop right before your eyes, except the picture is in your mind. In other words, what you are doing is shaping your dream into a vision!

My favorite definition of VISION comes from the great Irish writer, Jonathan Swift, who said *"Vision is the art of seeing things invisible to others."*

> *"Vision is the art of seeing things invisible to others."*
>
> — Jonathan Swift

A vision is nothing more than *a dream so clear, so vivid,* that nothing can discourage you from achieving it and no one can ever steal it from you.

If dreams are fuzzy, a vision is in sharp focus. When you have a vision, you see the place you want to be ... you taste it ... you walk around in it. Your vision becomes like a preview to a soon-to-be-released movie. When you have a vision, it's not a matter of IF your dream will happen. It's a matter of WHEN your dream will happen.

A Vision Worth $10 Million!

The comedian Jim Carrey, who starred in the hit movies *The Mask*, and *Batman Forever*, understands the power of a clear vision. During a career lull in the late '80s, Carrey dreamed about becoming rich and famous. He wrote down his dreams ... and then he crystallized his dream into a vision with a daring, creative gesture. He wrote himself a check for $10 million and postdated it to Thanksgiving Day, 1995. Now, that's what I call daring to dream!

Amazingly, in late November of 1995, Carrey was offered $10 million to star in *The Mask 2!* You'd have a hard time convincing Jim Carrey, who commanded upwards of $20 million a picture in 1996, that daring to dream was a waste of his time!

The Vision of Walt Disney

Another classic example of someone with a vision was Walt Disney. Here's a man who turned a cartoon mouse into an international, multi-billion-dollar enterprise! Walt's vision of creating a fantasy playground for children of all ages was so vivid, he converted thousands of acres of California farmland into the world's first successful theme park —Disneyland.

In fact, Walt Disney's vision was so strong, it endured even after his death. Walt Disney World in Orlando, Florida, wasn't near completion until long after Uncle Walt passed away. At the ground breaking ceremony for Walt Disney World, a reporter made the comment to Roy Disney, Walt's nephew, that it was too bad Walt wasn't alive to see his dream come to life.

Roy smiled at the reporter and said, *"Oh, but you're wrong. [Walt] Disney World was part of Walt's grand vision. Believe me, he saw all of this completed long before any of us."* Disney was an exceptional visionary because of his extraordinary ability to "see the invisible."

Solid Marriages Have a Shared Vision

A recent interview hosted by Dr. James Dobson on his popular radio show *Focus on the Family* validated the importance of creating a vision in your life. Dr. Dobson was interviewing a marriage counselor who had studied 100 successful marriages in order to discover what happily married couples have in common. According to the counselor, one of the key ingredients to a successful marriage is a *shared* vision.

The counselor observed that most young married couples start out dreaming, usually about having a family and owning their own home. Then, a few years down the road, they discover they've accomplished those dreams ... and then they make a fatal mistake. *They don't think up new dreams!*

Tragically, husbands and wives who stop dreaming together often start drifting apart. The marriage counselor concluded his talk with this statement: *"Without exception, successful married couples have a SHARED VISION they are always working toward."*

The marriage counselor's observation about the importance of a shared vision could also be said about businesses ... or about YOU, INC., for that matter. Visions are the vivid mental pictures that keep us on course. Without a shared vision, it's hard to stay focused and on track because you're not really sure where you are headed! The Book of Proverbs says it best: *"Without a vision, the people perish."*

> *"If you don't know where you're going, you're never gonna get there."*
>
> — *Yogi Berra*

That's why stage two, VISUALIZE YOUR DREAM, is so important. Without focusing your dreams into a vision, those dreams have a way of just drifting around aimlessly in your mind, without focus or purpose. What a waste!

Stage Three: Plan Your Dream

Stage three is to PLAN YOUR DREAM. The planning stage separates the participants from the spectators ... the drivers from the passengers. You see, when you start drawing up a plan for your dream, it shows you're serious. Planning means you've committed yourself to walking the walk ... instead of just talking the talk!

For example, what do you think would be the first thing a banker would ask for if someone requested a loan of $100,000 to start a new business. How about, *"Where's your business plan?"*

The banker knows from experience that new businesses without solid business plans seldom succeed. Why? Because anyone who would try to open a new business without taking the time to plan where they are going and how they will get there is planning to fail, plain and simple! Like Yogi Berra used to say, *"If you don't know where you're going, you're never gonna get there."*

Three Steps to Planning Your Dream

There are three steps you need to take to draw up a plan for realizing your dreams:

Step one is to write a personal mission statement.

Step two is to break your dreams down into goals.

Step three is to write daily TO DO lists.

Let's take a look at each one of these steps in more detail, beginning with writing a mission statement for YOU, INC.

Step One: Write a Mission Statement for YOU, INC.

A mission statement is really nothing more than a written statement of your purpose in life. It could be a one-sentence statement, like a slogan. Or it could be a couple of paragraphs. That's up to you.

No matter what the length, a mission statement has the power to inspire people to levels of achievement they never dreamed possible. One of the most powerful mission statements in history is also one of the shortest. It's only three words long. But those three words literally lifted a Fortune 500 company out of a decade-long slump.

The three words come from a Bob Seger song that anchors perhaps the most successful TV ad campaign in history. The words are "LIKE A ROCK" ... and amazingly, those three simple words helped GM rebuild its image ... improve its product ... and instill a sense of pride in every worker building a Chevy truck. In the words of Kurt Ritter, manager for Chevy trucks, *"LIKE A ROCK captures the soul of our division. It is how to build a truck. It is how to run a company."*

The mission statement for my publishing company, INTI

Publishing, isn't very long either. Only one sentence. But it sets the direction for everything we do. Here's what it says:

"The mission of INTI Publishing is to empower the average person to recognize the enormous value of personal development and the vast benefits of free enterprise through quality books, tapes and seminars."

We refer to this mission statement almost daily because it reminds us of who we are and what we should be doing with our time and talents. If an author comes to us and asks us to publish a book about growing award-winning roses, I suggest they try a different publisher, because a book about roses, no matter how good it is, doesn't fit in with our mission statement! Without a clearly defined mission statement, we could be drifting all over the place, like a boat without a rudder.

My Personal Mission Statement

Let me ask you a question: Would you agree with me that you should never ask someone to do something that you're not willing to do yourself? Likewise, I wouldn't ask you to write a mission statement for YOU, INC. if I had not written one for myself. Here's my YOU, INC. mission statement:

"My mission in life is to put my God-given talents to good use every day; to improve my relationships with God, my family and my friends; and to give back more than I take."

I cover a lot of territory with that mission statement, to say the least. But it helps me focus my life by reminding me what's really important. I've been told by friends, for instance, that I can be generous to a fault, especially when it comes to picking up the tab at dinner. But that's one of the ways I give back ... and I'm a firm believer that what goes around, comes around.

The best way to write a mission statement for YOU, INC. is to ask yourself, *"What's my purpose in life?"* Your answer will pretty much describe your mission statement.

Perhaps the following hypothetical situation will illustrate the importance of setting goals and planning the dreams for YOU, INC.

What would you think if you were researching companies to work for, and you came across a company that had no mission statement ... no monthly or yearly sales goals or production goals ... no goals for new product development ... and no goals for improving employee benefits? Is this the kind of company you'd want to work for? Of course not!

Likewise, why would a company want to hire someone who had no mission statement, no career plan and no specific goals? Would you hire a person like that? Then why would anyone want to hire you if your company, YOU, INC., had no dreams ... no vision ... and no goals?

Step Two: Write Down Your Goals

I think most people don't have written goals because *they tell themselves* they don't understand how to go about writing them. Frankly, that's a cop-out!

The REAL reason people avoid writing down goals is because they fear they won't be able to live up to them. Secretly they think, "If I write down a goal and don't accomplish it, that will mean I'm a failure." That kind of thinking is like the overweight, smoking columnist saying you shouldn't make resolutions because you'll break them anyway! THAT'S NONSENSE!

Look, you — and only you — are responsible for YOU, INC., isn't that true? That means YOU are responsible for your dreams.

YOU are responsible for your vision.

YOU are responsible for writing down your mission statement.

And YOU are responsible for writing down your goals.

All you need to get started is a pencil, paper and a few guidelines outlined on the next two pages.

Setting Goals for the "Five Fs"

First of all, you need to take out five sheets of paper and then print in big letters at the top of each page the "Five Fs." The Five Fs are as follows:

One, *Faith* ....
Two, *Family* ....
Three, *Friends* ....
Four, *Finances* ....
And five, *Fitness*.

Now, on the left side of each of the five pages, write down these phrases:

LONG-TERM GOALS (3-5 years)

SHORT-TERM GOALS (6 months to a year)

IMMEDIATE GOALS (30 days)

Now you're ready to write down your goals. All you need to keep in mind is that goals need to be specific, measurable, challenging and have a completion date.

For example, you may be 40 pounds overweight, and your dream is to lose 40 pounds and keep it off. Here's the way you would break that dream down into long-term goals .. short-term goals ... and immediate goals:

LONG-TERM GOALS

I will reach my ideal weight and maintain that weight within five pounds.

SHORT-TERM GOALS

I will lose 40 pounds over the next 12 months, which is less than four pounds a month — or one pound per week.

IMMEDIATE GOALS

I will limit the number of calories I consume to 2,000 a day;
I will walk 20 minutes every morning before breakfast;
and I will lose two pounds by Sunday night.

Now do you see how you can break down a dream into specific, measurable and dated goals?

To-Do Lists

Just as you need to break your dreams down into specific goals, you need to break those goals down into a daily TO-DO LIST. I'm such a big believer in a daily to-do list that I had a printer design and print several thousand of them.

I use these every day and give them as gifts to my clients. And I must say, I get more productivity out of my to-do list than I do from any other business tool, with the possible exception of the telephone. I swear, with a telephone ... a fax machine ... and a to-do list, you could conquer the world!

I'd like to conclude our discussion on the principle of DARE TO DREAM with a true story that perfectly illustrates how *thinking* ... *visualizing* ... *and planning* your dreams can dramatically increase the value of YOU, INC.

A Girl Scout's Dream Come True

The story concerns a girl scout named Markita Andrews, who dreamed a big dream and then made it come true!

> *"We all live under the same sky ... but we DO NOT all have the same horizon."*
>
> — *Konrad Adenauer*

Markita and her mother had always dreamed about traveling around the world. They'd often talk about their dream, and Markita's mother, who worked as a waitress, would often say to her, "*I'll work hard and put you through college. Then you can make enough money to take us around the world, fair enough?*"

When Markita was 13 years old, she read in her Girl Scout magazine that the girl who sold the most cookies would win a trip around the world for two, all expenses paid.

Suddenly Markita's *dream* began to take shape into a *vision* ...

She could *visualize* herself selling boxes and boxes of cookies ...

She could *visualize* herself receiving first prize ...

And most of all, she could *visualize* herself and her mom traveling throughout Europe ... the Orient ... the entire world!

Even though she was only 13 years old, Markita instinctively knew that thinking and visualizing her dream wasn't enough. She knew she needed to map out a specific plan.

So with the help of her mother and her aunt, Markita began to develop a plan. Here are some of the guidelines they wrote down for Markita during their early planning sessions:

1. When you are doing business, dress for business, which means always wear your Girl Scout uniform on sales calls.

2. Always ask for a big order, especially on Friday night.

3. Always smile, always be nice, and don't accept the first "no."

4. Don't ask people to BUY your cookies. Ask them to INVEST.

Each day after school Markita changed from her school clothes into her Girl Scout uniform and started knocking on doors. When people answered, she would smile, look them directly in the eye and recite her mission statement to them:

"Hi, I'm Markita Andrews and I have a dream. I'm earning a trip around the world for me and my mom by merchandising Girl Scout cookies. Would you like to invest in one dozen or two dozen boxes of cookies?"

Selling Cookies Leads to Disney Movie

In one year's time, Markita sold 3,526 boxes of Girl Scout cookies and won her trip around the world. Over the next few years she went on to sell more than 42,000 boxes of cookies ... starred in a Disney movie about her quest ... and co-authored a best-selling book called *How to Sell More Cookies, Condos, Cadillacs, Computers ... and Everything Else!*

Is it fair to say that Markita Andrews dramatically increased the value of her YOU, INC. by daring to dream? ... and by setting up a plan to make those dreams happen? I have to believe the answer to that question is a resounding YES!

Now think about this for a moment. If a 13-year-old Girl Scout can accomplish her dream of traveling around the world with her mom, what can you accomplish by daring to dream? The sky's pretty much the limit, isn't it? As the diplomat Konrad Adenauer once said, *"We all live under the same sky ... but we DO NOT all have the same horizon."*

Expand Your Horizon by Dreaming Big Dreams

Why not expand your horizons by daring to dream? The worst that could happen is that you aim for the treetops ... fall short of your dreams ... and only clear the fence. But folks, by failing to clear the treetops, you would have succeeded in clearing the fence, isn't that true?

And I want to assure you that on the other side of that fence is a big, wonderful world full of endless opportunities just waiting to be discovered ... on the other side of that fence is a wonderful world of endless adventures just waiting to be experienced.

If only you ... DARE TO DREAM!

• • •

PRINCIPLE 3: _____
The Power of Belief!

It is better to die for something than to live for nothing.
— Dr. Bob Jones, Sr.

You've probably heard Henry Ford's famous observation about belief: Ford said, and I quote, *"If you think you CAN ... or if you think you CAN'T ... you're right!"*

I love that quote because it sums up the essence of belief. If you think you can do something, well ... you're right. YOU CAN! But if you think you CAN'T DO THAT VERY SAME THING, guess what? You can't!

Amazing, isn't it, that more often than not, people will succeed not on the basis of their merits, but on the basis of their belief?

I've always been fascinated by people with an unshakable belief in what they're doing. Time and again throughout history, people with a strong belief in themselves and their mission have accomplished amazing feats, despite what the masses of people — and often even the experts — said to the contrary! Here are four legendary figures who illustrate just what I mean.

Vincent van Gogh

Vincent van Gogh sold only two paintings while he was alive — and both of those were to his brother! Despite savage criticism from fellow artists who said his artistic technique was primitive, van Gogh believed in his talent and his vision. Ironically, today the hundreds of colorful, vibrant paintings he couldn't even give away in his lifetime are worth nearly a billion dollars!

Fred Astaire

At Fred Astaire's first screen test, the testing director at MGM

Studios wrote a short memo to the studio head indicating that Astaire didn't have what it takes to succeed in motion pictures. Here's what the memo said:

"*Can't act. Can't sing. Can dance a little.*"

Astaire went on to star in scores of classic song-and-dance movies, and American audiences are forever indebted to Fred Astaire for believing in himself and pursuing his dream.

> "*If you think
> you CAN ...
> or if you think
> you CAN'T ...
> you're right!*"
>
> *— Henry Ford*

Margaret Mitchell

Margaret Mitchell published only one book in her lifetime ... but oh, what a book it was! *Gone with the Wind* won the Pulitzer Prize in 1939 and became perhaps the most-watched movie in history.

What most people don't know is that *Gone with the Wind* was turned down by 32 publishers! Although a very shy, private person, Mrs. Mitchell believed so strongly in her book that she kept knocking on doors until a publisher finally saw what the other 32 publishers missed!

Albert Einstein

Albert Einstein was such a late bloomer that his teachers thought he was mentally retarded! Einstein didn't speak until he was four years old, and couldn't read until he was seven. One teacher described him as "mentally slow, unsociable, and adrift forever in his foolish dreams." He was such a lackluster student that he was expelled from one college and refused admission to another!

Fortunately, Einstein believed more strongly in his own abilities than in all the negative assessments from some of his teachers. Einstein, of course, developed into one of the great thinkers of the 20th century, and his Theory of Relativity is so intellectually challenging that only a handful of people living today can fully comprehend it!

When I hear stories like these where people triumphed because they believed in themselves, I always think of Eleanor Roosevelt's observation that *"No one can make you feel inferior without your consent."* Certainly, the people in these examples didn't cave in at the first negative comments from short-sighted critics. If they had, the world would be a much poorer place. They "kept on keeping on" because they believed in themselves!

The great thing about belief is that you don't have to have the smarts of an Einstein or the talent of Fred Astaire to enjoy the tremendous benefits! Where is it written that only legends have a lock on the power of belief? Folks, I'm here to tell you that the simple principle of belief can work wonders for YOU, INC., too! All you have to do is believe!

> *"No one can make you feel inferior without your consent."*
> — *Eleanor Roosevelt*

I-Believe-It Box

Dr. Robert Schuller, in his best-selling book *Power Thoughts*, talks about a successful executive who keeps an "I-Believe-It" Box on his office desk. Anytime the executive comes across a project that just won't move forward — like a stalled sales contract or a difficult proposal — he just tosses it into the I-Believe-It Box, closes the lid and lets it sit there for a couple of days.

Two days or two weeks after tossing the item into the box, the executive takes a new look at it. In the executive's own words, here is how the belief box works:

"Somehow, when I return to the item a few days later, I see something I didn't see before. I think of a new way to attack the problem. I jot it down, and if it still doesn't move where I want it to, back in the box it goes. Amazingly, it always works! Since I've been using the I-Believe-It Box, I haven't lost one sale, one project or one proposal!"

. . . .

This is a great story because it documents the power of belief! Always remember: *"What the mind can conceive ... and the heart can BELIEVE ... you can achieve."* The I-Believe-It Box is just one person's way of reminding himself on a regular basis the awesome power inherent in the principle of belief.

The Bible's Definition of Belief

Everybody is familiar with the concept of belief, but if pressed to define it, we'd probably struggle a bit. The best definition of belief I know is the same as the Bible's definition of faith: The Book of Hebrews defines faith — or belief — in these words: *"Faith is the substance of things hoped for ... the evidence of things not seen."*

In other words, you don't have to "see it to believe it," as the old saying goes. When you TRULY believe in something, your belief is evidence enough. You see the vision in your mind so clearly that you know it's just a matter of time before it becomes a reality. That's what belief is all about.

> *"Change your mental habits into BELIEF instead of DISBELIEF. In so doing, you bring everything into the realm of possibility."*
> — Dr. Norman Vincent Peale

The Power of the Placebo Effect

In fact, belief is so powerful, it can actually *create* an outcome! The medical phenomenon of the placebo effect is the perfect example. A placebo is a harmless, unmedicated pill used in controlled tests to determine whether or not an experimental medicine works against a specific disease.

One group of patients receives doses of the drug being tested. The other group receives the placebo. Because both groups *believe* they are receiving medicine that will cure their illness, the condition of some of the patients who have taken the placebo starts improving.

In other words, the placebo effect occurs when a patient *believes* in a doctor, treatment or medicine so completely that the mind tells the body to heal itself!

Most doctors will tell you that placebos work for about 35 percent of the patients. But a recent review of 15 years of medical articles indicates that up to *70 percent* of patients in some studies said they had received significant relief from placebos! Amazing, isn't it, that people can literally cure themselves of illnesses just through the power of belief!

In his classic book, *The Power of Positive Thinking*, Dr. Norman Vincent Peale had this to say about belief: *"Change your mental habits into BELIEF instead of DISBELIEF. In so doing, you bring everything into the realm of possibility."*

The Power of Positive Thinking

Dr. Peale knew firsthand what he was talking about, for his own life served as living proof that positive thinking can work wonders. Peale lived to the ripe old age of 95 ... and up until the age of 93, he was delivering more than 100 speeches a year to audiences around the country.

For 54 years he hosted a weekly radio program, and he authored 46 books and delivered a sermon every Sunday for more than 50 years. Ironically, as a young man Peale suffered from what he called "the worst inferiority complex of all," and he originally developed his positive thinking philosophy to help himself!

Evidently, millions of people from all over the world are eager to learn about Dr. Peale's empowering I CAN message because his book, *The Power of Positive Thinking*, has sold more than 20 million copies in 41 languages since it was first published in 1952! My greatest wish is that the rest of the world's four billion-plus people could hear Dr. Peale's inspiring message about approaching life with an I CAN attitude, instead of an I CAN'T attitude!

Self-Fulfilling Prophecies

Unfortunately, the opposite happens when people think negative thoughts ... when they take an I CAN'T approach to life. Recent scientific research proves that negative beliefs can, in fact, cause negative consequences! For instance, researchers in England reported that the risk of being involved in an automobile accident went up as much as *52 percent* on Friday the 13th! The scientists proved what I've been saying all along — that beliefs can be so strong they become self-fulfilling!

I Can vs. I Can't

Have you noticed there's a lot more I CAN'T thinking (I prefer to call it "stinkin' thinkin'") going on than I CAN thinking? Certainly there are a lot more negative stories on TV and in the newspapers than positive ones. I don't pretend to know all the reasons people are attracted to negativity. Maybe it's human nature. Maybe it's the fact we hear the word NO about seven times more often than we hear the word YES.

All I know is, there are a lot more pessimistic people in this world than optimistic people. There are a lot more people who believe they CAN'T do something than people who believe they CAN. And that, my friends, is unacceptable!

So how do we go about taking Dr. Peale's advice and "Change your mental habits into belief, instead of disbelief?" The answer is, we start with ourselves ... we start by working on the belief system of YOU, INC., instead of blaming all of our woes on THEY, INC. We start by getting I CAN'T thinking out of our lives and replacing it with I CAN thinking! And there's no better time to replace I CAN'T thinking with positive thinking than today ... right now ... right this moment!

A Funeral for I Can't

My favorite story about replacing I CAN'T thinking with I CAN thinking comes from the book *Teacher Talk* by Chick Moorman. The story concerns a fourth grade teacher named Donna who devised a creative way for her students to stop thinking in terms of I CAN'T and start thinking in terms of I CAN.

One morning early in the school year, Donna asked her class of 31 students to take out a clean sheet of paper and write the words I CAN'T in big capital letters at the very top of the page. Then she asked the students to make a list of all the things they couldn't do. Here's what some of them wrote:

"I can't do 10 push-ups."

"I can't eat only one cookie."

"I can't do long division with more than three numerals."

" I can't get Debbie to like me."

While the students labored away on their lists, the teacher was busy making her own list, such as:

"I can't get Alan to use his words instead of his fists."

"I can't get John's mother to come in for a teacher conference."

When the lists were completed, Donna asked the students to fold them in half and drop them in the empty shoe box on her desk. Once all the papers were collected, Donna put the lid on the box, tucked it under her arm, and instructed the students to follow her out the door. On the way down the hall, Donna stopped at the custodian's room and grabbed a shovel, and then led her students out the door and onto the playground.

Donna marched the students to the farthest corner of the playground. Turning toward them with a solemn expression, Donna announced, *"Children, we are gathered here today for a very serious occasion. We are going to bury I CAN'T."*

She then proceeded to dig a hole in the ground. The digging took 10 minutes because all of the kids wanted to have a turn. By the time each child had dug out a shovel-full of dirt, the hole was three feet deep. Donna gently placed the box of I CAN'Ts into the bottom of the freshly dug grave.

A Eulogy for I Can't

Then she turned to her students and asked them to form a circle around the grave, join hands and bow their heads. Here is the unforgettable eulogy Donna delivered:

"Friends, we gather today to honor the memory of I CAN'T. While he was with us on earth, he touched the lives of everyone ... some, more than others. His name, unfortunately, has been spoken in every public building — schools, city halls, state capitols and, yes, even our White House.

"Today we have provided I CAN'T with a final resting place. He is survived by his brothers and sisters — I CAN ... I WILL ... and I'M GOING TO RIGHT AWAY. They are not as well known as their famous relative ... and are not as strong and powerful yet. Perhaps someday, with your help, they will make an even bigger mark on the world.

"May I CAN'T rest in peace ... and may everyone present pick up their lives and move forward in his absence. Amen."

Then Donna and her students filled in the fresh grave before returning to the classroom, where they celebrated the passing of I CAN'T. As part of the celebration, Donna cut out a large tombstone from butcher paper and wrote in big, black letters these words:

I CAN'T
MAY HE REST IN PEACE
MARCH 28, 1980

This paper tombstone hung in Donna's classroom for the rest of the year. Whenever one of her students forgot and said "I CAN'T," Donna would point to the tombstone. More often than not, the student would smile and rephrase the statement.

Now I ask you, isn't that a delightful story? You know, I've never had the pleasure of meeting the teacher in this story, but I guarantee you, I'd enroll my children in her class in a heartbeat if she were teaching at the local elementary school!

Just think how much people could accomplish if they'd hold a mental funeral for all their I CAN'Ts! I'm telling you, if that happened, you'd see a dramatic increase in the stock of every YOU, INC. in the world!!

Believe in Others, Not Just Yourself

So far in this chapter we've talked about belief in yourself. And without a doubt, believing in yourself is crucial if you want to dramatically increase the value of YOU, INC. The simple fact is, if YOU don't believe in YOU, how do you expect *anyone else* to believe in you?

Belief in yourself is essential, that's for sure. But there's more to life than just you, no matter how independent you are. As the great English poet John Donne noted hundreds of years ago, "No man is an island." Which means you've got to believe in something ... and somebody ... outside yourself.

Without exception, great achievers believe in themselves, and they believe in other people. No matter how much Columbus believed in himself, for example, he couldn't have made a successful voyage to the New World without believing in his crew.

Truly successful people believe in their families ... they believe in their friends ... they believe in their country ... they believe in their causes ... and last but not least, truly successful people believe in something larger than all the world and all its people put together. They believe in God!

Now let's take a look at how believing in things outside yourself can enrich you and dramatically increase the value of YOU, INC. Leo Durocher, the fiery manager of the New York Giants in the 1950s, is the perfect example of how believing in others is essential for your own personal success.

Believing in a Rookie Named Willie

Early in the 1951 season Durocher promoted a 20-year-old minor leaguer named Willie Mays to the starting position in center field. Durocher knew talent when he saw it, and he had all the faith in the world that Mays would become a superstar.

But the shy young ball player from a small town in Alabama was awestruck playing before huge crowds in major league stadiums. Mays was so nervous he went hitless in his first 12 times at bat. After finally managing a hit, he went hitless for another 14 straight at bats!

The young outfielder was devastated! At the conclusion of yet another hitless game, Durocher found Mays crying in the dugout. Between sobs Mays said, *"Mr. Leo, I can't hit the pitching in the majors."*

Durocher put his arm around the heart-broken youngster and said evenly, *"Willie, as long as I'm manager of the Giants, you're my centerfielder."*

Sure enough, the next day Durocher started Mays in center field, and his belief was rewarded. Mays collected two hits that afternoon. For the rest of the year Mays hit well over .300, and he went on to become a perennial all-star for the next 20 years! You see, even when Willie Mays didn't believe in himself, Leo Durocher believed in him. And that belief dramatically increased the value of both individuals.

Just imagine. The Hall-of-Famer who went on to accumulate more than 3,000 hits and 600 home runs ... started his career with only one hit in his first 26 attempts!

The Benefits of Belief

Common sense tells you there's real power in believing in others, whether they are co-workers ... family ... or friends. In fact, recent research bears this out.

Doctors at Dartmouth Medical School charted the progress of 232 elderly patients who had undergone open heart surgery. The researchers discovered that the patients who did NOT participate regularly in social groups — whether it was a church supper group, a seniors club or a fraternal group — were three times more likely to die within six months of their surgery. In the words of one of the senior researchers, *"Having a strong faith and being embedded in a web of relationships like churchgoing have definite health benefits."*

Instead of prescribing Valium and anti-depressants like candy, perhaps doctors should start writing a prescription that says, "GO TO CHURCH EVERY WEEK."

The long and short of it is this: People who believe in God and in a cause larger than themselves are healthier ... happier ... and more successful than people who don't. End of subject.

The Person with the Strongest Belief Wins!

I sincerely believe that the person with the strongest belief wins.

Think about it. Christianity won out over paganism during the days of the Roman Empire. Democracy won out over fascism in World War II. Capitalism won out over communism in the cold war. Why? Because our belief in God ... and our belief in the causes of freedom and free enterprise were stronger than theirs! It's like the story of David and Goliath.

> *"One person with belief is worth 99 who only have an interest."*
>
> — *John Stuart Mill*

When David volunteered to fight the giant, everyone around David told him he was crazy. They told David that Goliath was so huge there was just NO WAY he could win. To which David replied, *"Goliath's so huge, there's no way I can miss!"*

You see, David was a believer of the first order. He believed in himself ... he believed in God ... and he believed in his cause. Now, this is NOT to say David was without fear. Of course he was afraid. According to the Bible, Goliath was more than nine feet tall ... was covered from head to toe in armor ... and was a seasoned survivor of numerous hand-to-hand combats. But David's unshakable belief empowered him to overcome his fears and triumph over Goliath and the non-believers.

The philosopher John Stuart Mill summed up the awesome power of belief with these words: *"One person with belief is worth 99 who only have an interest."* The Biblical account of David's victory is certainly proof of that statement.

Believe in Yourself and Your Cause

I've noticed over the years that successful people and unsuccessful ones receive about the same amount of negative feedback. It's just that the successful people — the Henry Ford's of the world — don't buy into what the dreamstealers say, whereas unsuccessful people do.

It's like the old expression, "If you don't stand for something, you'll fall for anything." If people don't passionately believe in themselves ... their families ... their country ... and their cause ... they can be easily swayed by the first new thing that comes through the door.

I'd hate to think where I would be today if I had listened to everyone outside myself instead of listening to my own inner voice telling me to hold true to my beliefs. When I told friends and acquaintances I was writing a book, for example, most of them laughed at me. You see, I was a C student at best in English throughout high school and college. I've always been a lousy speller and my grammar is average, at best.

People would say, *"What do you know about writing books — you've never written a book before."* My answer to that comment was, *"If the first guy who ever wrote a book thought like that, there wouldn't be any books."* I figured if my critics didn't think they could write a book, that was their business. But that didn't mean I had to buy in to their story!

You see, I believed in myself and my cause. I truly believed I had something to say that other people needed to hear. I knew beyond a shadow of a doubt that I could deliver a message that people would find valuable ... interesting ... and useful.

My critics were focusing on the minor things — the grammar and the spelling and my grades in school. On the other hand, I was more concerned about the major things, like delivering the message and organizing it in a way that made it easy for people to understand. I figured I could always find an English teacher or an editor to clean up the small stuff. That's why I've adopted the expression, *"Don't major in the minor things,"* as my personal motto!

Well, I'm proud to report that more than one million copies of my first book, *Who Stole the American Dream?*, were sold in less than three years. How many copies would I have sold if I had believed in my critics instead of my cause and my abilities? I'll tell you how many — ZERO!

The Making of a Living Legend

I'm sure you've heard the name Arnold Palmer. Since 1955 Palmer has won scores of professional golf tournaments, including four Masters Tournaments. He's a living legend, and one of the most famous people in the world.

So, what was the secret to Palmer's success? I've got to believe that, more than any other single factor, it was his unyielding belief in his ability to get the job done. Anyone who's ever seen Arnold Palmer swing a golf club would say he is not the most graceful golfer to ever play on the tour.

But when he settled over a ball on the first tee ... or crouched over a birdie putt ... he *believed* he was going to hit the ball right where he wanted. In the game of golf, where confidence and belief are everything, Palmer ruled!

Although he's won hundreds of tournaments and awards, his office is simple and virtually empty of trophies, except for one battered little cup that he received for his first professional win at the Canadian Open in 1955.

The only other adornment in his office is a small, framed plaque with an inscription that serves as a fitting closing to this section on the Power of Belief. Here's what the plaque says:

If you think you are beaten, you are.
If you think you dare not, you don't.
If you'd like to win but think you can't,
It's almost certain that you won't.
Life's battles don't always go to the stronger woman or man.
But sooner or later, those who win
Are those who think they can.

● ● ●

PRINCIPLE 4:
The Courage to Take Action

You don't drown by falling in the water.
You drown by staying there.
— Edwin Louis Cole

H ave you ever seen the movie *Moscow on the Hudson*, starring Robin Williams? It's a delightful comedy set in the 1970s about a Russian circus performer who defects to America while on tour in New York City.

Robin Williams' character is named Vladimir, and when we first meet him he's playing the saxophone in the Moscow Circus Band. Although in his early 30s, Vladimir lives with his parents in a cramped, run-down apartment in Moscow. His best friend, Anatoly, is a circus clown who dreams endlessly about defecting to America.

Action Speaks Louder Than Words

Both men end up in New York when the Moscow Circus plays Madison Square Garden. The two friends are dazzled by the wealth and freedom available to Americans, and Anatoly the Clown keeps up a steady conversation to his friend about defecting when he finally gets a chance.

Robin Williams' character, Vladimir, dreams of freedom, too, but he keeps reminding his friend of the realities of defecting: They don't speak much English ... They have very little money ... and the Russian secret service is watching their every move. If they tried to defect and failed, they would be sentenced to life in a Siberian prison camp.

A small window of opportunity to defect is opened when their bus to the airport stops for a 10-minute shopping trip at Macy's department store. At the end of the brief shopping spree, as the Russian secret service men are pushing everyone toward the exit, the two friends' eyes meet. Anatoly the Clown looks over at the secret service man, who has turned his back ... and then over to a Macy's security guard. Now is the time to act!

Suddenly, Robin Williams' character runs over to the security guard, throws his arms around him and shouts, "I DEFECT! HELP ME! I DEFECT!" The secret service men try to drag him back, but the Macy's security guard radios for the police.

When the dust settles, we see Russian secret service men desperately trying to persuade Vladimir to board the bus with the rest of the circus troupe. But the defector refuses. His dream of living in America is finally realized.

Heaven Never Helps the Person Who Won't Act

The camera cuts to the other circus performers staring solemnly out the bus windows. The camera pans down the the row of sad faces until it stops on a tear-streaked face pressed against the glass. It's the face of Anatoly the Clown, who didn't seize his opportunity when he had it.

> *"Heaven never helps the person who will NOT ACT."*
>
> — *Sophocles*

The lesson of this scene is what this section is all about — THE COURAGE TO TAKE ACTION! You see, Anatoly the Clown talked a good game, but when it came right down to it, he didn't have the courage to back up that talk with action.

Robin Williams' character, on the other hand, let his actions do the talking for him. Both men had the same dream ... to enjoy the freedom that America has to offer. In fact, Anatoly's dream for freedom was probably stronger than Vladimir's.

But only one of the two friends ended up living his dream ... the other didn't.

Only one of the two friends returned to a life of oppression and hopelessness ... the other didn't.

Only one of the two friends had the courage to act ... the other didn't.

"Heaven never helps the person who will NOT ACT," observed the Greek philosopher Sophocles more than 2,000 years ago. It just goes to show you that some things never change ... and that the key to success today is the same as it was 2,000 years ago. And it will be true for the next 2,000 years: ACTIONS speak *louder than words.* Always have ... always will!

You know, it's blatantly obvious to anyone with a lick of common sense that nothing happens without action. "For every action, there is an equal and opposite reaction" is one of the basic axioms of elementary physics. So, let me ask you a question. If it's common knowledge and a universal law that nothing really happens until someone or something takes action ... why is it that so many people spend so much time and effort avoiding action?

Procrastination: The Slow Death

I can answer that question with one word ... a word that a wise man once called "the natural assassin of opportunity." That word is PROCRASTINATION! I call procrastination "the slow death" because it starves action to death, rather than dealing it one fatal blow.

Tom Peters, in his best-selling business book *In Search of Excellence,* analyzed hundreds of companies in order to discover the key principles that drive America's best-run enterprises. After years of research, Peters came up with eight attributes that great companies have in common. Of those eight, the number-one attribute for excellence is — in Peter's own words — *"a bias for action."* In other words, the best companies don't just sit around and talk about doing something — THEY DO IT!

Peters went on to say that the mentality of management at mediocre companies is "let's study it some more ... that's not my department ... let's table that proposal until next quarter."

The battle cry of excellent companies is "DO IT, FIX IT, TRY IT — NOW!"

What about your company, YOU, INC.? Do you have a "bias for action?" ... Do you look for excuses to get off your assets and get something done? Or are you a procrastinator who never met a problem that couldn't be put off until tomorrow?

Frankly, I've never really understood procrastinators because I'm just the opposite. My motto has always been "fire, ready, aim" ... and while my impulsiveness sometimes gets me in trouble, at least I'll never die a slow death by procrastination!

Later? Why Not Now?

One of the classic anti-procrastination stories is about Benjamin S. Bull, the man who founded and ran Medal Gold Flour Company. During a meeting with the company's top managers, Bull asked a high-ranking officer to report on the status of one of Bull's pet projects.

The manager said his department hadn't gotten around to working on the project, but they would attend to it *eventually.* Bull was an impatient man, and in exasperation he jumped up from the meeting table, leaned over the startled manager and shouted, *"Eventually? Why not now?"*

The expression *"Eventually? Why not now?"* made such a profound impact on the Medal Gold management team that it was immediately adopted as the company's motto — and it remained the Medal Gold motto for more than 50 years!

The bottom line is you are better off *doing something* than JUSTIFYING *doing nothing* — so why not get busy doing something? Like I always say, "Ignorance on fire is better than knowledge on ice." *Just do it*, the Nike ads say. I couldn't agree more! JUST DO IT!

I believe people procrastinate because they feel that taking action is more painful than avoiding it. If people would spend as much time *taking action* as they do *thinking about how they can avoid taking action*, they'd be twice as productive in half the time. As

Abraham Lincoln was fond of saying, *"You can't escape the responsibility of tomorrow by evading it today."*

What Have You Done Today?

I came across an anonymous poem about procrastination that sums up what I'm saying. It's called *What Have I Done Today?*

I shall do so much in the years to come,
But what have I done today?
I shall give my gold in a princely sum,
But what did I give today?
I shall build a mansion in the sky,
But what have I built today?
It's sweet in idle dreams to bask,
But if not I, who shall do the task?
Yes, this is the question each soul must ask:
What have I done today?

What have I done today? That's a great refrain, isn't it? When you think about it, today is the only time you have to get anything done, because there's no guarantee you're going to see tomorrow!

My minister always reminds our congregation of the importance of living in the moment with this expression: *"Yesterday is a canceled check. Today is cash in hand. Tomorrow is a promissory note."*

When you think of time like that, you suddenly realize that the only thing you can take to the bank is the present ... so you might as well put it to good use by acting today — RIGHT NOW! It's like the Black and Decker commercial on TV that shows a man using his electric drill to put up some shelves. At the end of the ad the announcer says, *"There's more satisfaction in putting things up than in putting them off."*

Little Actions Add Up to Big Results

I think another big reason so many people become procrastinators is they think they have to accomplish a monumental task at one sitting. Nothing could be further from the truth.

The beauty of taking action is that small actions over time can get big results! During the next few pages you'll learn how small, consistent actions can yield big, big results in three major areas of your life — your money, your health and your time.

Small Savings Add Up to a Big Pension

First, let's take a look at how taking the action of saving a little bit each month can make you richer than you ever dreamed! Imagine that your goal is to retire with an income of $50,000 a year. If you were to begin saving just $100 a month in your early 20s — that's only $25 a week — and invest it in a mutual fund earning between 12 and 15 percent a year ... by the time you turn 65, you would have accumulated more than half a million dollars!

"No one ever got fat eating one big meal."

— old Chinese saying

Then at 65 you can start living off the interest — which would calculate to $50,000 or $60,000 a year — without ever having to touch the principal! And all it took was to pay yourself $100 a month, an amount that most of us wouldn't even miss if we got into the habit of putting it away before we spend it!

Walking Off Unwanted Weight

Now let's take a look at how small, consistent, daily actions can dramatically improve your health. Let's assume that, like most Americans, you could stand to lose a few pounds. What if there were a simple way to lose weight, gain fitness and enjoy the process? Does that sound like something you could get excited about? Well, there is ... and it's something we do every day. It's called walking. It's easy ... enjoyable ... and a great way to lose weight and improve your fitness!

Consider this: If you were to go for a brisk, 20- to 30-minute walk six days a week, either before work or on your lunch break, and then substitute an apple for that mid-afternoon candy bar, you could lose at least 10 ... maybe 20 pounds in a year's time!

It just goes to show you that you don't have to take major actions — like running 12 miles every day and living on raw carrots — to lose that tire around your middle. All you have to do is take small, daily actions to enjoy major benefits!

How to Add a Month to Your Year

Let's look at one more example of how small actions can deliver big dividends. How would you like to add another month to every year of your life? Impossible, you say? Not at all. Listen to this: If you set your alarm to wake you up a half hour earlier, six days a week, you'd gain an extra three hours a week ... three hours that you could use to read ... to exercise ... or to spend with your loved ones.

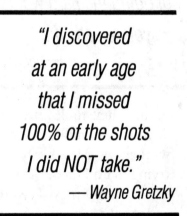

"I discovered at an early age that I missed 100% of the shots I did NOT take."

— *Wayne Gretzky*

You do that 52 weeks a year, and you've added 156 productive hours to your year. *That's the equivalent of adding almost a month of 40-hour weeks to your year!*

Now think about it. Over a lifetime, that extra half hour every day would add almost four years of 40-hour work weeks to your life! What would you do with that extra time? Exercise? ... play with your kids? ... work on YOU, INC.? Can you see how a small action, like getting up a bit earlier, can add years to your life ... and life to your years? That's what I mean when I say small, consistent actions can yield big results!

A Little Lost Time and a Lot of Lost Money

I recently read an article in a management magazine that documents how small actions can add up to huge proportions over time.

The story was about how the managers at Toyota were continually implementing new ways to make their operations more efficient and profitable.

The reporter noted that all the workers at one Toyota plant wore leather tool belts around their waists. He quickly calculated that if each tool belt cost $20, the company was spending upwards of $100,000 a year to keep workers in leather tool belts. The reporter approached one of the plant managers with the idea that the company could save money by cutting back on tool belts.

> *"Persistence is the hard work you do after you get tired of doing the hard work you already did."*
>
> *— Newt Gingrich*

The manager smiled and told the reporter that those tool belts were one of the best investments the plant ever made. You see, a Toyota engineer had calculated that if each worker at Toyota were to drop a screwdriver once a day ... and then took only a few seconds to pick it up ... it would cost Toyota $115 million a year in lost production time! With a tool belt, workers were less likely to misplace tools and spend unproductive time trying to find them. The tool belts may have cost Toyota thousands of dollars ... but they saved the company millions!

Isn't that an amazing story? Did you ever imagine that one small action that takes literally seconds — like dropping and picking up a screwdriver — could add up to the astronomical figure of $115 million?

All of these examples prove that you can get big, BIG results from small, consistent actions. The key isn't how big your action is. The key is taking consistent actions over time. It's like the old saying, "How do you eat an elephant? One bite at a time."

You Don't Shoot, You Don't Score

When a reporter asked Wayne Gretzky, the most prolific scorer in the history of the National Hockey League, the secret to his scoring more goals than anyone in history, Gretzky replied, *"I discovered at an early age that I missed 100 percent of the shots I did NOT take."*

In other words, if you don't shoot, you don't score. It's that way in life, just as it is in hockey. If you don't do it, it doesn't get done. Nothing, I repeat, NOTHING, takes the place of taking action! And the more action you take, the more results you get.

Look, it just stands to reason: If you want to be thin, you have to do what thin people do. If you want to be rich, you have to do what rich people do. More often than not it's a bias for taking action, not talent, that separates the big shots from the little shots. Truth is, a big shot is nothing more than a little shot who just keeps on shooting!

The Power of Persistence

There's a word for consistent, daily actions, you know. That word is persistence. And it's probably one of the most underused and underrated words in the entire dictionary. The best definition of persistence I've heard comes from Newt Gingrich, who says persistence is *"the hard work you do after you get tired of doing the hard work you already did."*

> *"Perseverance is not a long race. It is many short races one after the other."*
>
> *—Anonymous*

In other words, persistence may not be glamorous, but it sure gets the job done! I think too many Americans today overvalue talent and undervalue persistence.

We think that only the supertalented people make it big in this country — but nothing could be further from the truth. For every super-talented successful person, like Michael Jordan, there are thousands of successful people who made it on sheer guts ... determination ... and persistence.

Colonel Sanders of Kentucky Fried Chicken fame is a perfect example. Colonel Sanders didn't even start his world-wide enterprise until he retired from the railroad. When he was over 60 he started shopping his secret chicken recipe to restaurants all over the South. For months on end he drove thousands of miles, stopping at every roadside restaurant along the way, to see if the owner would buy his chicken recipe.

More often than not, Sanders ended up sleeping in his car because he couldn't afford a motel room. All in all, Colonel Sanders was rejected by nearly 500 places before a kind restaurant owner took pity on him and allowed him to demonstrate his process.

Today there are thousands of Kentucky Fried Chicken franchises in hundreds of countries all over the world. You can't tell me the reason Colonel Sanders became a household name was because he was the best cook in the world. And he wasn't the most brilliant businessman in the world, either. If he had been, he would have owned the railroad that employed him as a laborer for 40-plus years.

But he was, without a doubt, one of the most persistent people in the world. And it was persistence, not talent, that took him to the top of his profession.

A wise man once remarked, *"Perseverance is not a long race. It is many short races one after the other."* Think about it. In the confrontation between the stream and the rock, the stream always wins. Why? As Shakespeare put it, "Much rain wears down the marble." The simple truth of the matter is that consistent, persistent efforts will always triumph in the end.

The Prince of Popcorn

You've probably heard the name Orville Redenbacher. He was the skinny, gray-haired man wearing a red bow tie who sold his gourmet popcorn on TV. Redenbacher made millions from his popcorn. We'd all love to grin our way to fame and fortune selling something as profitable as popcorn. But what most people don't know is that it took Redenbacher more than 20 years and 30,000 popcorn hybrids before he was able to develop a fluffier, tastier popcorn.

It wasn't luck that made Redenbacher a success. And it wasn't working really hard for only a month ... or even a year ... that made the difference. It was persistent action over time that turned Redenbacher from a manager of a popcorn farm into a multi-millionaire!

Never Give Up, Never Give In

There's a Chinese folktale that perfectly illustrates the importance of persistence. In the folktale a holy man has a dream in which he is taken by the angels to visit heaven. As the angels escort the man through the heavenly mansion, they pass a huge room stacked from wall to ceiling with gifts.

The holy man stops and stares into the room, dazzled by the variety and beauty of the acres and acres of presents. *"Why are all these lovely presents stacked up in this room?"* the holy man asks the angels.

A beautiful young angel steps forward and with a sad sigh explains, *"This is the room where we store the things people have been praying for ... but, sadly, they quit praying right before their presents were to be delivered."*

You, know, when I see people giving up on themselves and their dreams at the slightest setback, my first reaction is sadness, just like the angel in the Chinese folktale. But sadness soon gives way to frustration ... because I hate to see capable people giving up and caving in. I think if more people *fully understood the power of persistence*, we'd accomplish so much more as individuals and as a nation than most of us ever dreamed!

Calvin Coolidge, for one, fully understood the importance of persistence, and his short dissertation on persistence bears repeating:

"Nothing in the world can take the place of persistence. Talent will not; nothing is more common than unsuccessful people with talent. Genius will not; unrewarded genius is almost a proverb. Education will not; the world is full of educated derelicts. Persistence and determination alone are omnipotent. The slogan 'PRESS ON' has solved and always will solve the problems of the human race."

Failure Was NOT an Option

Rich DeVos and Jay Van Andel, co-founders of The Amway Corporation, one of America's largest privately owned companies, are living

. . . .

testimonies to Coolidge's observation that persistence is the best way to accomplish your goals. In the early days of their company, Rich and Jay held nightly sales meetings. One of their first meetings was scheduled in Lansing, Michigan, and the hard-working partners spent the better part of two days promoting the event.

> *"You can make money,*
> *or you can*
> *make excuses.*
> *You just can't make*
> *them both*
> *at the same time."*
> *—Anonymous*

They ran ads on the radio ... they put notices in the newspaper ... they passed out brochures on the busiest street corners during lunch hour. They'd done their homework and were all set for a big turnout in the 200-plus-seat auditorium they rented for the evening.

Well, on the night of the big event, only two people showed up! Can you imagine, all that work ... all that money ... and only two people show up. Jay and Rich weren't just disappointed. THEY WERE DEVASTATED! *"What's going on here?"* they asked themselves. *"Are we banging our heads against a wall for nothing ... Or was this just one battle in a long war? Could our dream of building an international company come true? ... Or are we two grown men who should know better than to chase a fantasy?*

Here's what Rich DeVos had to say about that evening in his best-selling book, *Believe:*

"Did you ever make a rock-'em-sock-'em speech to two people in a room with two hundred seats in it? And then drive home at two o'clock in the morning because you couldn't afford to pay those motel rates? In situations like that, night after night, you do one of two things. Either you give up, or you persist. We persisted."

Because Rich DeVos and Jay Van Andel chose to persist in their dream, today they are two of the wealthiest people in America, worth billions of dollars each! That's proof positive that persistence pays off in a BIG WAY!

Making Excuses vs. Making Money

If the founders of Amway were looking for an excuse to give up on their dream, that incident in Lansing, Michigan, years ago would have been a perfect one. But they didn't. They weren't looking for excuses ... they were looking for results. As a wise person once put it, *"You can make money, or you can make excuses. You just can't make them both at the same time."*

Now, I'm well aware that most people have ready-made excuses about why they can't get up an hour earlier ... or why they can't save 10 percent of their salary every month ... or why they can't lose weight ... or why they can't exercise. All I know is this: The person who really wants to take action finds a way; the others will find an excuse.

How about you? ... Are you committed to getting what you want out of life by taking simple, consistent daily actions to improve YOU, INC.? Are you willing to become persistent in your efforts to get better in all phases of your life? Or are you like so many people who make excuses justifying why they're maxed out on their credit cards ... or those who justify why they're 40 pounds overweight?

Look, it's human nature to look for excuses to justify failure, rather than reach back when times are tough and do what you gotta do to get what you really want.

But excuses don't make the mortgage payment.

Excuses don't reduce your waistline from size 42 to size 36.

Excuses don't dramatically improve YOU, INC.

Excuses never got the job done ... and never will. Only persistence and determination get the job done. Like I always say, "There are reasons ... and there are results. And reasons don't count!"

No Excuses in the Hall of Fame

Do you think Hank Aaron would have broken Babe Ruth's home run record if he called in sick every time his shoulder hurt? Do you think Cal Ripken, Jr. would have broken Lou Gehrig's consecutive games played record if he sat out a game every time he had a bad cold or a sprained ankle? Not a chance!

Both Ruth and Ripken became record setters because, for them, taking action and getting the job done took priority over taking the easy way out by making an excuse. These two legends never avoided taking action because it took too much effort.

Taking action was something to look forward to because it challenged their physical talents and mental toughness. Perhaps that's the reason Babe Ruth is a Hall-of-Famer and Cal Ripken is destined for Cooperstown when he retires!

Don't Let Regrets Take the Place of Your Dreams

At the beginning of this section I shared a story with you about Vladimir the saxophone player and Anatoly the Clown. Both men started in the same place, working for the Moscow Circus. But sadly, they didn't end up in the same place! The one who had the courage to take action, Vladimir, ended up free to shape his own destiny in America.

The one who lacked the courage to take action, Anatoly the Clown, ended up back in the Soviet Union, living a dreary life of mediocrity ... repression ... frustration ... and pain.

Friends, don't allow yourself to become like Anatoly the Clown, who had the opportunity to change the course of his life ... but didn't ... Don't allow your regrets to take the place of your dreams.

Have the courage to take control of your life.

Have the courage to take charge of your fate.

Have the courage to ... TAKE ACTION!

• • •

PRINCIPLE 5:
Attitude Is Everything

*No one ever developed eyestrain looking
on the bright side of things.*

— Anonymous

A friend of mine is fond of saying, *"Everybody lights up a room. Some when they enter ... some when they leave."*

I love that line because it's one of those small truths that all of us can relate to. We love cheery, optimistic people because they light up our lives with their positive enthusiasm and passion.

We love being around them because their attitude is contagious, and we want to catch it! No question about it, people with great attitudes light up a room when they enter it!

We also know the opposite types — you know the kind ... sour, negative people who take pleasure in raining on our parade. Unfortunately, their attitude is catching, too. It seems that people with bad attitudes just aren't happy unless they're unhappy. They brighten up a room *when they leave* because they take their dark view of the world with them.

What You See Is What You Get

One of my favorite stories about attitude is about a wise old gatekeeper living in 18th-century Europe whose job was to greet the new visitors to a bustling Mediterranean city located on a busy trade route.

Travelers entering the city would stop to ask the old man directions and to inquire about the availability of work. One day a traveler stopped at the gate and inquired of the gatekeeper, *"Old man, what are the people like in your city?"*

The old man paused to scratch his head before replying, *"What were the people like in the town you came from?"*

The traveler scowled and said dryly, *"A terrible lot. They are mean-spirited, greedy and dishonest."*

"Well," replied the gatekeeper with a nod of his head, *"you'll find them the same in our city. Don't say I didn't warn you."*

About an hour later another traveler approached the city gates. Judging by his dress and facial features, this traveler appeared to be the younger brother of the previous traveler.

The old man spoke first, saying, *"Judging by your looks, young man, it must have been your brother I spoke to earlier. Are you looking for him?"*

The young man smiled and shook his head no, answering, *"No, not on your life, old man. You see, my brother has a most sour disposition. I'm sad to say I don't miss his company in the least."*

The young man approached the old gatekeeper, offered a handshake, and asked, *"If you could answer my question, gatekeeper, I would be forever indebted. Judging from your age, you must know many people in this city. In your esteemed opinion, sir, what are the people like in your city?"*

The old man paused to scratch his head before replying, *"What were the people like in the town you came from?"*

The traveler smiled and with joy in his voice replied, *"Oh, there can be no finer people. To a man they are honest, hard-working and generous to a fault. I hated to leave, but lack of opportunity drove me to seek my fortune elsewhere."*

"Well," replied the gatekeeper with a smile, *"you'll find them the same in our city. We welcome you with open arms!"*

The moral of the story is that when it comes to attitude, what you **choose to see** is what you get. People with bad attitudes **choose to look at the world through dark glasses** tinted with cynicism; as a result, they mostly see only suspicious-looking people lurking in the shadows.

People with good attitudes, on the other hand, **choose to look at the world through rose-colored glasses** tinted with optimism; they mostly see friendly people laughing and playing in the sunshine.

Some People Are Never Happy

Playing golf is a perfect example of how your attitude can color your view of the world. If you've ever played golf, you know exactly what I'm talking about. I love to play golf, and I often play with golfers who are much, much better than I am. On a good day, many of my friends can shoot in the 70s. I'm more likely to shoot in the high 80s, however.

But even when I play poorly and shoot in the high 90s, I still find ways to enjoy myself. To me, shooting a good score is only a small part of the enjoyment of golf. The other part is enjoying the beauty of nature ... enjoying the company of friends ... or enjoying the thrill of hitting a great drive or making a long putt.

Some of my friends, however, make themselves miserable unless everything is going their way! If they make a par, they grumble about missing their opportunity to make a birdie. If they shoot a 38 on the front nine, they're unhappy because they missed shooting a 36. Amazing as it may sound, some people could be playing on the most beautiful day of the year on the most beautiful course in the world, and they'd be miserable!

That's what I mean when I say it's your choice whether you wear dark, cynical glasses ... or whether you wear bright, optimistic glasses. You — and only you — determine the world view of YOU, INC.

Now let's take a closer look at this thing called "attitude" to see what it really is ... and then let's look at how your attitude can dramatically affect the value of YOU, INC.

The Definition of Attitude

Attitude can be defined as *"a mental filter through which we process our thoughts and view the world."* Given the fact that the average person has more than 50,000 separate thoughts per day, it's obvious that the expression *attitude is everything* is true, indeed!

People who filter their thoughts through a negative screen will view the world as a dark, ominous place populated with gloom and doom. Filter those same thoughts through a positive screen, and the world is a bright, adventure-filled place overflowing with surprises and opportunity.

So then, what does it mean when we say someone has a positive or "good attitude" versus a negative or "bad attitude"? Let's take a few minutes to compare and contrast some of the common traits of people with good and bad attitudes so we have a better understanding of attitude and how it affects not only us, but everyone around us.

Good Attitude vs. Bad Attitude

Here's my list comparing bad attitudes to good ones:

A bad attitude blames others when things go wrong.

A good attitude accepts responsibility for making mistakes.

A bad attitude makes excuses.

A good attitude gets results.

A bad attitude says, "Get going."

A good attitude says, "LET'S get going."

A bad attitude looks at life as a trial to endure.

A good attitude looks at life as an adventure to enjoy.

A bad attitude looks at a rose bush and sees the thorns.

A good attitude looks past the thorns ... and sees the roses.

Now I ask you, after reading this list, which kind of person would you prefer to work with — a person with a good attitude ... or a person with a bad attitude? More to the point, which person would you prefer to be? The one with the good attitude ... or the one with a bad attitude?

True-Life Stories Prove Attitude Is Everything

Let me share with you some true-life stories that perfectly illustrate why a good attitude is not just important — it's essential to improving your fair market value! These stories paint a vivid picture that remind us of this simple truth: A good attitude can be the only thing that separates tragedy from triumph.

Apollo 13 Mission

The first story involves the Apollo 13 mission to the moon back in 1970. Very few people remember how close the crew was to being stranded in space when the Apollo 13 spacecraft started breaking apart in mid-flight. Then in 1995, the movie version of the Apollo 13 mission brilliantly recreated the drama and heroics surrounding that event.

The Apollo 13 mission to the moon was deep in space and progressing according to schedule when an oxygen tank explosion cut off the electrical current to the command module. Suddenly, there was a real possibility that the three-man crew would be stranded in space 100,000 miles from Earth with no hope of rescue.

Within minutes of the first explosion, the situation turned even worse, as one system after another in the spacecraft started to fail. At Mission Control in Houston, scores of scientists stared at their consoles in shock and disbelief. Control Central was in a near-panic!

Only the quick work of the flight director, Gene Krantz, held the team together, as one piece of equipment after another went on the blink. Krantz calmed the panicked scientists and reassured the stunned flight crew with this one sentence: *"What have we got on the spacecraft that's good?"*

That question refocused the group to think in terms of *what was working instead of what was broken* ... that question changed the group attitude from "we're doomed" to "let's pool our knowledge and come up with a plan to save our mission."

Mission Statement for a Good Attitude

In essence, the question *"What have we got on the spacecraft that's good?"* could serve as a mission statement for a good attitude. The power of Krantz's question is that it challenged everyone involved in Apollo 13 to become part of the solution, instead of part of the problem!

This story proves that, in times of crisis, a positive attitude isn't just important — it's absolutely crucial! By focusing on the positives instead of the negatives during setbacks — whether they are financial or physical or emotional — we position ourselves to end up as winners instead of losers.

Amazing Invention Saved by Edison's Attitude

Thomas Edison, the great American inventor, is yet another example of what can happen when we focus on the positives instead of the negatives during setbacks. When Edison was 67 years old, his factory was virtually destroyed by a late-night fire and much of his lifetime's work went up in smoke. To make matters worse, the buildings were insured for only $238,000, even though the damage exceeded $2 million!

> *"Friends, there is great value in disaster. Look, all of our mistakes have burned up. Thank God we can start anew."*
>
> — *Thomas Edison*
> *after a fire burned his laboratory to the ground*

The next morning Edison walked around his grounds surveying the smoldering ruins. Friends and family gathered around the old man, offering their regrets and condolences. Edison summoned all of the visitors to his side and addressed their concerns with these words:

"Friends, there is great value in disaster," he said evenly. Gesturing toward the gutted concrete buildings, Edison said, *"Look, all of our mistakes have burned up. Thank God we can start anew."*

Just think, if Edison had taken a negative view rather than a positive one, he could have used the fire as an excuse to give up, and the world would have missed out on one of his greatest inventions.

For miraculously, only three weeks after the fire, Edison introduced an invention that would bring pleasure to hundreds of millions of people ... an invention that would go on to revolutionize the entertainment industry. That invention was the world's first phonograph!

Oh, What a Beautiful Morning

Oscar Hammerstein, the great American lyricist who collaborated on scores of classic musicals like *Oklahoma* and *The King and I*, summed up the power of a great attitude with these words:

"I know the world is filled with troubles and many injustices. But reality is as beautiful as it is ugly. I think it is just as important to sing about beautiful mornings as it is to talk about slums. I just couldn't write anything without hope in it."

A Real-Life Superman

The last story I want to relate to you is a tragic study in irony, for it involves a man who played the role of Superman in the movies — Christopher Reeve.

In many ways, Reeve was a real-life superman. He was energetic and athletic. He was an accomplished actor. He piloted his own jet airplane. He was an expert skier. He owned horses and entered jumping events near his home in Virginia.

Tragically, that all changed on May 27, 1995, at a horse-jumping event. Reeve was negotiating to jump over a fence on his thoroughbred when the horse stopped short. Reeve was leaning forward in preparation for the jump, and when the horse stopped, Reeve was thrown over the horse's neck.

His head hit the ground first, knocking him unconscious. By the time the medics reached him, he was totally limp, as if the life had gone out of him. The fall had shattered his spinal cord, leaving him totally paralyzed, unable to move his arms and legs, or even to breathe without the aid of a respirator.

Making a New Life While Making a Difference

Now, if there were ever an excuse to give up on life, wouldn't you agree that total paralysis would have to rank near the top? And, yes, there was a brief time after his accident that Reeve wanted to give up and end it all.

But once he realized the outpouring of love and support from his family and friends, his positive attitude took over. Christopher Reeve made the choice to make the best of his situation. He made the choice to turn a negative into a positive.

Today, he focuses on what he CAN do, rather than his limitations, and he is concentrating his efforts on raising money to find a cure for spinal injuries. In his own words, he is dedicating his life to helping others less fortunate than him and he feels lucky that he's in a position to be a positive influence.

> *"Your friends will stretch your vision ... or choke your dreams."*
> *—Anonymous*

When I hear stories like these, I'm compelled to ask, "If people like Thomas Edison can find the good in a catastrophe ... and people like Christopher Reeve can remain upbeat in the face of a life-altering tragedy, how can other people justify whining and complaining about insignificant events in their daily lives?"

Isn't it amazing how people allow themselves to become angry and upset over little inconveniences, like getting caught in a traffic jam ... or having to take out the trash? Sadly, too many of us get caught up in the little day-to-day problems in our little corner of the world, and we lose perspective on what life is really all about.

Putting Things into Perspective

You may think that times are tough and you have it rough — but compared to what? You may think you're down on your luck — but compared to whom? Sure, all of us have storms pass through our lives from time to time. We can't direct the wind, that's for sure. But we can adjust the sails.

Let's be honest with ourselves by putting things into perspective: Is it really tougher to be a single mother working at McDonald's today than it was to be an immigrant wife working in the Chicago stockyards in 1915? Is it really tougher to lose a job to corporate downsizing today than to be an Oklahoma farmer during the Dust Bowl years?

Yes, life can be unfair. Bad things happen to good people. But it's also true that whining about it doesn't make it any better. In fact, whining makes things worse because it validates the negative instead of seeking out the positive.

> *"You can get better ... or you can get bitter."*
>
> —Anonymous

Celebrating National Whiner's Day

I truly believe this country would be a lot better off if we just got all of our whining out of the way at one time so we could all concentrate on making our lives more productive. A Methodist minister, Reverend Kevin Zaborney, went so far as to organize a National Whiner's Day back in 1986. Zaborney suggests we set aside the day after Christmas to get all our whining out in preparation for the New Year.

The minister was making fun of our growing national preoccupation with whining and complaining, of course. But the concept makes a lot of sense: Set aside one day to wallow in the negatives so that we can be positive the other 364 days of the year!

You Can Get Better ... Or You Can Get Bitter

Please realize that this chapter isn't the place to get into what causes a person to have a positive attitude as opposed to a negative one. I don't pretend to be a psychiatrist. My purpose in this program isn't to analyze the causes. My purpose is to encourage you to more fully understand the enormous benefits of having a positive attitude and to make you aware that you — and only you — are in control of your attitude. As the old saying goes, *"You can get better ... or you can get bitter."* I'll take better over bitter any day, how about you?

You don't have any control over lots of things in life. You can't control, for example, how tall you are. You can't control the color of your eyes or your skin. Those characteristics are hereditary. They're stamped onto your genes, and there's nothing you can do to change that, so you may as well accept it.

> *"A mirror reflects a man's face, but what he is really like is shown by the kind of friends he chooses."*
>
> — The Living Bible, Proverbs 28

Your Friends Are Your Board of Directors

But, you can choose your attitude, thank goodness. You can choose what you feed your mind, like the books you read and the TV shows you watch. You can choose your friends. You can choose which people you will listen to and emulate and which ones you will ignore.

A wise person once said, "Your friends will stretch your vision ... or choke your dreams." That's why it's important that you pick your friends carefully.

Choose Your Friends VERY Carefully

Just as a successful company must carefully select its board of directors, you must carefully select who sits on the board of directors for your personal company — YOU, INC.

I can't emphasize too much how important it is to select friends with good attitudes to sit on your board. Can you imagine a Fortune 500 company selecting a problem drinker who is always blaming someone else for his troubles to sit on its board? Not a chance! Successful companies seek out successful directors with the skills and contacts that can help make a good company even better.

So doesn't it make sense to treat YOU, INC. the same? If you hang out with people who have lousy attitudes, guess what — you're going to have a lousy attitude! If you hang out with drunks and losers who haven't grown personally or professionally since high school, what does that say about you?

Proverbs 28 in *The Living Bible* says it this way: *"A mirror reflects a man's face, but what he is really like is shown by the kind of friends he chooses."*

I've heard my mother say the same thing thousands of times in slightly different words: *"Tell me who you hang out with, and I'll tell you who you are"* is the way my mom put it. No matter how you say it, it all boils down to the same thing. You are who you associate with, so if you want to become a better person, associate with better people.

> *"There is little difference in people — but that little difference makes a big difference. The little difference is attitude. The big difference is whether it is positive or negative."*
> — *W. Clement Stone*

Rid Your Life of Toxic People

If you are sincere about wanting to dramatically improve the value of YOU, INC. in all phases of your life, you must choose your friends carefully. If some of your so-called "friends" have negative attitudes and bad habits that hold you back, you need to get them out of your life.

I call people with bad attitudes "toxic people," and just as you would take special precautions to rid your home of toxic chemicals before they could harm you and your family, you must do the same with toxic people in your life!

That doesn't mean you shouldn't try to reach out to negative friends and relatives. Certainly you should do your level best to encourage your loved ones to grow. But it seems like some people have both feet cemented in a bad attitude, and it's not your responsibility to join them in their permanent pity party. If that means spending less time with your toxic "old" friends and spending more time with uplifting "new" friends, so be it.

Choose to Be Somebody

Look, life isn't a dress rehearsal. You only go around once. This is YOUR life ... YOU, INC. is YOUR company, no one else's! If some of your friends want to run their companies from a bar stool ... or if they want to put their minds in cold storage, that's their choice. But when they ask you to serve on their board of directors, I suggest you politely decline the invitation.

W. Clement Stone, a devoted follower of Dr. Norman Vincent Peale's philosophy of positive thinking and the founder of a hundred-million-dollar-a-year insurance company, summed up the importance of attitude this way:

> *"There is little difference in people — but that little difference makes a big difference. The little difference is attitude. The big difference is whether it is positive or negative."*

I'd like to end this discussion of *Principle Number Five: Attitude Is Everything* with an anonymous poem entitled *Somebody*. In a few short lines, this poem says about all that needs to be said on the topic of attitude.

Somebody did a golden deed;
Somebody proved a friend in need;
Somebody sang a beautiful song;
Somebody smiled the whole day long;
Somebody thought, "It's sweet to live;"
Somebody said, "I'm glad to give;"
Somebody fought a valiant fight;
Somebody lived to shield the right;
Was that "somebody" ... you?

• • •

PRINCIPLE 6:
Develop Productive Habits

Winning is a habit. Unfortunately, so is losing.
— Vince Lombardi

O ne of my favorite writers is John Grisham, the best-selling author of *The Firm, The Client* and *Pelican Brief.* Because of the fabulous success of his books, Grisham is a millionaire many times over today. But the road leading to his fame and fortune was anything but a superhighway. Fact is, it was more like a winding dirt road filled with dead-ends and potholes!

Finding Reasons to Write a Book

Before becoming a full-time writer, Grisham was a lawyer. Like most successful lawyers, he put in long hours at the office, often 60 hours a week, sometimes 80! Despite his grueling schedule, Grisham wanted more than anything to write a novel.

However, Grisham had countless ready-made excuses as to why he could NOT write a book — excuses like the fact he had no "creative" writing experience ... that he had obligations to his wife and two kids ... that he didn't have the time because he was working 10 hour days, six days a week ... that he was under incredible stress at work.

But Grisham knew that when it was all said and done, he had a choice. He could either *find reasons* TO write a novel...or he could find reasons **NOT TO** write a novel ... and then justify to himself why he couldn't do it. Fortunately for his readers and his family, Grisham chose to find reasons **TO** write his first novel.

He wrote his first book, *A Time to Kill,* by making one simple adjustment in his life. He changed his morning habits. He started getting up at 5:00 a.m. and working on his novel. In effect, he didn't have enough time in his day to write. So he *made the time* by getting up a couple of hours earlier each day. Less than one year later, Grisham had a completed manuscript to send to publishers.

Word of Mouth Saved the Book

Only one problem. The first publisher said, "Thanks, but no thanks." So did the second ... and the third ... and the fourth ... and so on. But Grisham was determined to see his book in print, so he kept submitting his book until, finally, publisher number 26 said "yes!"

The publisher had so little faith in the book that only 5,000 copies were printed. At the time it seemed like 4,000 too many! The book was a bomb.

So Grisham made another choice. He decided to market the book himself. He bought 1,000 copies and then made it a habit to spend his weekends visiting every bookstore ... library ... and garden club meeting within driving distance of his home. It took months before his habit of giving talks and signing books on weekends began to payoff.

Slowly, over time, readers started recommending the book to friends. Word of mouth kept building and building until, finally, after nearly a year's worth of weekend personal appearances, John Grisham's first novel, *A Time to Kill*, exploded onto the best-seller list, where it stayed for 100 weeks!

To date there are more than 10 million copies of Grisham's first novel in print, and publishing houses and Hollywood studios pay him millions for the rights to his newest book, months before the first word has even been written!

Change Your Habits and You Can Change Your Life

This story emphasizes the importance of developing productive habits. Grisham was able to accomplish what he did because he changed his habits. He did what he had to do to turn his dream into a reality. He understood that he had to make some adjustments to his normal routines if he were serious about writing a novel. So he did just that by changing his sleeping habits.

Can you see how Grisham's new habit of getting up at 5:00 a.m. — let's say two hours earlier than normal — allowed him to accomplish a life-long dream? Just look at how developing the habit of adding two productive hours a day can make a world of difference. Over the span of a year, you could add 15 work weeks (or almost 4 months) of productive time to each and every year of your life.

Even if you woke up only 30 minutes earlier each day, you could add a month of 40-hour work weeks to your year! Isn't it astounding that developing a habit as simple as getting up a little earlier each day could have such a profound affect on your life? John Grisham is living proof of just that!

Your Habits Decide Your Future

Now, at first glance, habits appear to be small, harmless routines that help us personalize each day and give our lives a sense of structure and continuity. Because our habits are so predictable, they comfort us — especially in times of stress.

But not all of our habits are small ... or harmless. In fact, when it's all said and done, who we are — and what we become — is the sum of our good habits and our bad habits ... the sum of our productive habits and our unproductive habits ... the sum of our big habits and our little habits. As a wise man put it, *"Men do not decide their future. They decide their HABITS ... and their habits decide their future."*

> *"Men do not decide their future.*
> *They decide their HABITS ...*
> *and their habits decide their future."*
> *—Anonymous*

Grisham decided to make a habit of rising early and writing every morning before going into the law office. In turn, that habit decided his future. Today Grisham is no longer practicing law. He's a full-time writer doing what he loves while earning 100 times what he would be earning as a lawyer. And it all started with one small, daily, productive habit.

Dictionary Definition of Habit

Before we go on, let's take a moment to define the word *habit* so we all have a clear understanding of what habits are and how they significantly impact our lives.

According to *Webster's New World Dictionary*, a habit is *"an acquired pattern of action that is so automatic it's difficult to break."* Let me repeat this definition because it's rich with meaning. A habit is *"an acquired pattern of action that is so automatic it's difficult to break."*

Unfortunately, for most people, the word *habit* has a negative connotation, mainly because we've been conditioned to concentrate on the *"difficult to break"* part of the definition. That's what we think of when we use phrases like "smoking habit" ... "drinking habit" ... "drug habit" ... and "habitual offender."

But we need to remind ourselves that habits don't have to be bad or unproductive. It's obvious that people who acquire productive habits are far more likely to become successful ... and fulfilled ... and in control ... than people who acquire unproductive habits.

In fact, that's the message that Steven Covey gets across in his best-selling book, *7 Habits of Highly Effective People*. Covey spent years studying successful people in order to identify the behaviors that effective people have in common. Covey was the first person to point out the awesome power of effective habits and to communicate the idea that effective habits can be learned and taught to others.

Getting Stuck in a Rut

Let me paint a picture for you that will give you a better understanding of how our habits determine the direction of our lives. A friend of mine used to go on hunting expeditions in undeveloped areas of the Canadian Northlands. Every July my friend and a couple of his buddies would jump in a four-wheel-drive truck and head for the Northlands. He often joked that the Northlands were so cold they only had two seasons — winter and July.

The Northlands didn't get much traffic, so the roads were narrow and unpaved. In July the dirt roads began to thaw, and as the traffic picked up, each passing vehicle would dig a deeper rut in the muddy road. By the end of the short summer, the mud ruts would be several feet deep. Once the long winter set in, the ruts would freeze as hard as cement.

According to my friend, the frozen ruts on one of the back roads got so deep that the park service posted this sign at the entrance to the road: *"Driver, please choose carefully which rut you drive in, because you'll be in it for the next 20 miles."*

Well, our habits are like those ruts in the Northlands roads: They're easy to get into ... but very hard to get out of. In fact, don't we sometimes refer to our repetitive, unproductive behavior as "being in a rut?"

That's why it's imperative that we increase our awareness of the long-term benefits of choosing productive habits over unproductive ones. That's why you need to choose each of your habits very carefully, because you may have that habit for the rest of your life!

Are Your Habits an Asset, or a Liability?

As founder, president, and 100 percent stockholder of YOU, INC., you are responsible for developing productive habits that will increase your short-term and long-term value. Because our habits are either an asset or a liability to YOU, INC., we must nurture productive habits ... and we must work on replacing unproductive habits with productive ones.

To understand the impact that habits have on our lives, I want you to imagine that you are an employer seeking to hire a new person to fill a key position with your company. What kind of habits would you want that person to possess?

Would you want a well-organized employee who had the habit of managing his time wisely .... or someone who was always missing deadlines because he had a habit of putting off the big jobs until the last minute?

Would you want a well-read employee who had the habit of reading professional journals and business books at home in the evening ... or someone who had a habit of watching TV until bedtime?

Would you want a considerate, courteous employee who made a habit of giving each customer top-notch service ... or someone who had the habit of being short-tempered and abrupt with customers?

Obviously, every employer would prefer employees who have great work habits ... who have productive personal habits ... as opposed to workers who have self-limiting ... or even self-destructive habits.

Great People Cultivate Great Habits

I've got to believe that if you were to examine the day-to-day lives of history's most productive people, you'd find people who chose habits that encouraged productivity, rather than interfered with it.

If Lincoln, Ford and Edison were alive today, for example, do you think they would make a habit of coming home, flopping down in front of the TV, and then channel surfing until they fell asleep in their recliners?

The truth of the matter is that each of us has the power to turn just about any human endeavor into a productive habit. The key to dramatically improving YOU, INC. is to turn productive endeavors into new habits, and to replace our bad habits with good ones.

Replacing Bad Habits with Good Ones

Abigail van Buren, the writer of the widely syndicated advice column Dear Abby, says this about bad habits: *"A bad habit never goes away by itself. It's always an undo-it-yourself project."*

What Abby means is that bad habits are hard to break. That's why I don't recommend that people focus their time and efforts on breaking a bad habit. Instead of suggesting that people QUIT a nonproductive habit, I encourage them to REPLACE their nonproductive habits with productive ones!

For instance, wouldn't you agree that it's relatively easy to trade in the *unproductive habit* of listening to music in your car while you're commuting to work ... for the *productive habit* of listening to self-improvement audios, such as audios on time management, effective communication and so on? Wouldn't your new habit make you wiser and more knowledgeable? Of course — it's only good, old common sense!

Taking Inventory

What I'm encouraging you to do is to become *aware of how your habits affect your life* ... for awareness is the first step to replacing unproductive habits with productive ones.

Once John Grisham, for example, became *aware* that his habits were not helping him accomplish a life-long dream, he started thinking about which habits were moving him toward his goals ... and which ones were holding him back. That awareness led to his acquiring the habit of rising earlier each day and writing during those added hours.

> *"A bad habit never goes away by itself. It's always an undo-it-yourself project."*
>
> — Abigail van Buren

The best way to increase *your awareness* of your habits is to do what John Grisham did — sit down and take inventory of your existing habits. Think about which habits help you move forward, and which ones hold you back. Then think about the habits that could help you accomplish your dreams and goals in life. Finally, look for opportunities to substitute productive habits for unproductive ones.

Productive Habits vs. Unproductive Habits

Let's take a moment to look at some common, unproductive habits that many people *choose* to adopt. Then we'll look at some productive habits that could easily be substituted for the unproductive ones. Here's my short list of several common, unproductive habits and a productive substitute:

Unproductive Habit: Spending all your spare time in front of the TV.

Productive Habit: *Reading books that will expand your mind and improve your skills.*

Unproductive Habit: Pulling out your charge card to buy things when you don't have the money in the bank..

Productive Habit: *Paying cash whenever possible.*

Unproductive Habit: Reaching for a Hershey bar every time you're hungry.

Productive Habit: *Snacking on apples and fresh vegetables between meals.*

Unproductive Habit: Winding down from a stressful day by "relaxing" with four or five cocktails.

Productive Habit: *Managing your stress and reducing your blood pressure by exercising after work.*

Unproductive Habit: Always procrastinating and putting things off until the last minute.

Productive Habit: *Taking action and developing a sense of urgency about important projects.*

Making it a habit to save money every month is a perfect example of what I'm talking about. Let's say your dream is have enough money to retire comfortably at age 60 without ever having to work again.

For most Americans, that's NOT an unrealistic dream. But to realize that dream, you'd have to make it a habit to plan wisely and save religiously. If you are serious about wanting to retire in comfort, you can't choose to practice unproductive spending habits and expect to accomplish your goal.

Make Planning for Your Retirement a Habit

The results of a recent survey in *USA Today* paint a pretty dreary picture of most people's priorities in life. The survey said that American adults spend 16 times more hours shopping for clothes than they spend planning for retirement. According to the survey, Americans spend less than 10 hours A YEAR planning for their retirement ... but more than 145 hours a year selecting their wardrobe!

Wouldn't you agree this is a good example of poor time-management habits? You better believe it! Given the fact that Americans have the lowest savings rate of any industrialized country in the world, I'd have to say we need to take a long look at our spending and savings habits, wouldn't you agree?

Managing the Greatest Hotel in the World

I'd like to take a moment to share a true story with you that pretty much sums up what I mean when I talk about the importance of developing productive habits.

The story took place near the turn of the century in a small hotel in Philadelphia.

A young, ambitious clerk named George was determined to work his way up to a top management position in the hotel industry. Early in his training, George decided that the key to success in the hotel business was to put the customer first, no matter what the circumstances.

> *"When you gain control of your habits, you gain control of your life."*
> — *Burke Hedges*

So he made a conscious decision to develop two life-long habits: One, he would make it a habit to learn everything he could about the hotel business; and two, he would make it a habit to see that every customer's request was handled quickly and courteously. As a result of these two habits, George was making a name for himself with the owners, who were grooming George for a management position.

No Room at the Inn

One cold, rainy night while George was working the night desk, an elderly, well-dressed couple entered the lobby. The elegant gentleman approached the front desk and asked in a distinctive English accent, *"Young man, all of the big hotels are filled up, and my wife and I are desperate for a room. Could you possibly accommodate us?"*

George explained to the gentleman that there were three conventions in town, and that there wasn't a single vacancy anywhere in the city. As he surveyed the disappointed looks on their faces,

George reminded himself of his habit of putting the customer first, no matter what. As the elderly couple shuffled toward the door, George called out:

"Excuse me, sir. I wouldn't think of sending a nice couple like you out in the rain at one o'clock in the morning. We have no vacancies, but perhaps you would consider sleeping in my room this evening."

When the couple declined his offer, George insisted, saying that he wouldn't be needing the room anyway, seeing how he was on duty until the next morning. *"I'd rather have you occupy my room than have it sit vacant all night. Please, take my room. It's the least I can do for nice people on such a nasty evening."*

Not a Laughing Matter

The next morning, as the elderly man paid his bill, he handed George a substantial tip, smiled and said, *"Young man, you are the kind of manager who should be the boss of the best hotel in the United States. Maybe someday I'll build one for you."*

The young clerk looked at the charming couple, and all three of them had a good laugh at the old man's joke. Then George helped them carry their bags to the street and chatted with the delightful couple until their cab arrived.

> "No one ever went broke saving money."
>
> —H. Jackson Brown

Two years passed, and George had forgotten about the incident. His great attitude and great work habits had led to several promotions at the hotel, but George was getting restless. He felt he knew the hotel business inside and out, and he had his sights set on becoming a general manager.

One day he received a letter postmarked from New York City. It was from the elderly gentleman George had accommodated on that rainy night two years ago. The letter requested that Geoege pay a visit to him and his wife. Enclosed in the letter was a round-trip ticket to New York City.

In New York, the old man asked George seemingly endless questions. He wanted to know where George was from ... how long had he been in the hotel business? ... how would he run a major hotel if he were in charge? ... what were his goals and aspirations? ... and so on. George answered the questions courteously, and thanked the man for his genuine concern.

Dreams Can Come True

Then the old man led George to the corner of Fifth Avenue and 34th Street and pointed to a marvelous new building, a huge palace of reddish stone, with turrets and watchtowers thrusting high into the sky.

With a twinkle in his eye, the old man turned to George and said, *"This is the hotel I have built for you to manage."*

George burst out laughing, and congratulated the old man on his joke. Although the old man was smiling, he wasn't laughing. *"I assure you, young man,"* said the elderly man. *"I am not joking. I call this hotel the Waldorf-Astoria, after a long-standing family name. And you, sir, are the hotel's first manager. Congratulations!"*

You see, the old man's name was William Waldorf Astor, the heir to one of the largest fortunes in American history. The young clerk was George C. Boldt, who became the first manager of the grandest hotel of its time. To this day, the Waldorf remains one of the leading hotels in the world, with a small suite costing upward of $350 a night!

Productive Habits Are Like Seeds

The moral of the story is that productive habits are like seeds. The habits that we share today may not bear fruit immediately. It may take years for that fruit to ripen. But rest assured, productive habits will bring about productive results.

If George had not developed the productive habits of taking every opportunity to learn about his business ... if George had not developed the productive habit of satisfying every customer request, do you think he would have been chosen to manage the most prestigious hotel in the country? Not a chance!

But George knew instinctively that since we're creatures of habit anyway, it just makes common sense to adopt productive habits instead of unproductive ones. Likewise, each of us needs to examine our life and decide how we can turn everyday activities into productive habits.

Productive People Choose Productive Habits

When it's all said and done, you — and only you — are in charge of your habits. You choose them ... you cultivate them ... and you reap what you sow. That's why it's imperative that the habits you develop for YOU, INC. are assets, not liabilities.

> *"By perseverance, the snail reached the ark."*
>
> — *Charles Haddon Spurgeon*

By taking a look at people's habits, you get a good idea of what they value and what takes priority in their lives. When we choose our habits, what we are really doing is choosing how we spend our time, right? The truth is, time may be our most precious commodity, for once it's gone, we can never get it back. So why is it that so many people take time for granted, and just throw it away on mindless, meaningless activities?

A Nation of TV Addicts

For example, did you know the average American male watches almost 28 hours of TV a week? As a nation, the time we're wasting in front of the TV has reached ridiculous proportions — and I assume that most people aren't watching the Discovery Channel!

Just think of it this way: If a person is in the habit of watching four hours of TV every night, they're wasting more than 100 potentially productive hours every month ... which calculates to be almost *eight months of forty-hour work weeks every year!*

Amazing, isn't it? Just think how much they could improve YOU, INC., if they'd use that time to learn a new skill ... or to speak a foreign language ... or to improve their health by exercising!

It's my firm belief that productive people have productive work habits, plain and simple. We're all given the same number of minutes in each hour ... the same number of hours in each day ... the same number of days in each week ... and the same number of weeks in each year. Yet some people accomplish more in one year than others accomplish in an entire lifetime.

Little Habits Can Add up to Big Results

Remember the definition of habit? A habit is an *acquired pattern of action*, correct? You'll also recall from Principle Number Four — *The Courage to Take Action* — that actions don't have to be big to get big results. They just have to be consistent.

That's really the key to effective habits, isn't it? A productive habit is nothing more than small, consistent actions that add up to big, positive results. Let me give you an example of how a small, productive habit can lead to astonishing results.

Did you know that the typical consumer in this country carries a credit card balance of $1,750 at an annual interest rate of 18 percent? How long do you think it will take to pay off this balance if the consumer pays just the minimum of two percent on the unpaid monthly balance? Are you sitting down?

The answer is ... 22 YEARS AND NEARLY $4,000 IN INTEREST! Just imagine, by paying the minimum each and every month, you'd pay more than twice as much in interest as you borrowed — and you could raise a child from birth to adulthood in the process! Talk about a license to steal!

Now, let's say this same consumer develops the habit of paying an extra $25 each month. That's less than a dollar a day, so it's certainly not a huge sacrifice, wouldn't you agree? Now here's the amazing part. By paying just an additional $25 per month on the unpaid balance, *you would cut your payment time by 19 years!*

Just imagine, you could pay off your bill in only three years and four months, instead of 22 years. And you'd pay only $588 in interest instead of $3,647 in interest. Unbelievable, isn't it? And to think all you'd have to do is get in the habit of paying an extra $25 per month!

How Your Habits Become Your Destiny

The simple truth of the matter is this: Once you gain control of your habits, you will gain control of your finances.

Once you gain control of your habits, you will gain control of your health.

Once you gain control of your habits, you will gain control of your time.

Once you gain control of your habits, you will gain control of your relationships.

In short, once you gain control of your habits, you will gain control of your life.

Always remember, whatever you make a habit of is what you become. If you make a habit of winning — you're a winner! If you make a habit of giving — you're a giver.

YOU, INC. is a combination of your thinking habits ... your speaking habits ... your time-management habits ... and your performing habits. Those habits will determine whether YOU, INC. grows into a company that people admire and seek to invest in ... or whether YOU, INC. falters and is forced into personal bankruptcy.

I'll end with a short, anonymous maxim that describes better than I ever could how our habits are forever connected to our destiny like links in a steel chain. The maxim goes like this:

Be careful of your thoughts, for your thoughts become words.

Be careful of your words, for your words become actions.

Be careful of your actions, for your actions become habits.

Be careful of your habits, for your habits become your character.

Be careful of your character, for your character becomes your destiny.

• • •

PRINCIPLE 7:
Manage Your Emotions

Courage is mastery of fear, not absence of fear.
— Mark Twain

It seems like not a day goes by that we don't read or hear about a husband or a wife leaving their spouse for someone they "met" — and I use that word loosely — on the Internet.
Pretty astounding, isn't it, that two people, perhaps thousands of miles apart, meet accidently in cyberspace ... they communicate by sending electronic messages through their computers ... and then they decide to run off together even though they've never even met in person.

Doesn't it just boggle your mind to think that two grown adults would make a major, life-altering decision based almost solely on emotion?

We Make Our Decisions Based on Emotion

Amazing as it sounds, when you examine the way people make almost every decision in their lives, scenarios like this one are actually the rule, and not the exception. Students of human nature — from psychiatrists to novelists to religious philosophers — all agree that human beings make their decisions based on their emotions, and then justify those decisions with reason and logic ... rather than the other way around.

The great English satirist and poet, Alexander Pope, observed this phenomenon approximately 300 years ago when he wrote this couplet:

The ruling passion, be what it will
The ruling passion conquers reason still.

Pope understood that it was human nature for people to make

decisions based on emotions rather than reason. And like it or not, there's not much we can do to change human nature. We can't change the fact that Adam and Eve made an emotional decision to take a bite out of the forbidden fruit.

The Power of Emotions

Does that mean we're doomed forever to be ruled by our emotions? Of course not. But it does mean that, in order for us to manage our emotions effectively, we need to better understand the power of emotions so that we can run our emotions, rather than have our emotions run us.

> "The ruling passion, be what it will.
>
> The ruling passion, conquers reason still."
>
> — Alexander Pope

Let's take a few moments to talk about the power of emotions and how they profoundly affect our lives — sometimes for the better ... but all too often, for the worse.

First, let's look at the downside of emotions, which is certainly easy enough to document. All you have to do is crack open a great novel ... or a play by Shakespeare ... or a history book ... or the Bible at any given page — and you'll come face to face with the dark side of human emotions.

History is loaded with case studies of individuals — even whole nations, for that matter — whose "ruling passions conquered their reason," the most notable example being Hitler and the German people in World War Two.

Hitler in the 1930s and '40s — and Bosnia in the 1990s — are living proof of what can happen when people fail to manage their emotions. When emotions like greed ... envy ... prejudice ... and hate dictate terms and assume dominance over our intellect, disaster is inevitable!

Conquered the World, But Not His Emotions

One of the greatest figures in ancient history, Alexander the Great, is a perfect example of an exceptionally talented human being who was undone by his emotions. By the time Alexander the Great was 29 years old, he'd conquered the known world. By all accounts he was brilliant ... handsome ... courageous ... and ambitious.

Yes, Alexander the Great mastered the whole world ... he was king of kings on earth. But he had a fatal flaw — he couldn't master his emotions. Deeply depressed because there were no new worlds to conquer, Alexander the Great — the man who ruled the world before his thirtieth birthday — died a drunk at the age of 32!

From the days before recorded time when Cain killed his brother Abel out of jealousy ... to the fourth century B.C. when Alexander the Great drank himself to death out of despair ... to the 20th century when the Menendez brothers murdered their parents out of greed, decisions based on emotions have undone the best, and the worst, of God's children.

The Consequences of Unmanaged Emotions

Just take a look at your own life. Think about all the countless times you made major decisions based more on emotion than reason. Can you remember back to your high school days when you made some decisions without thinking them through? Fortunately, most of the emotional decisions we made as teen-agers turned out all right in the end ... and we laugh about them today.

But what about the high school kids who make the tragic emotional decision to jump in a car and drag race after drinking a few beers? All too often their failure to manage their emotions ends in a tragic car accident.

The point is, the consequences of *unmanaged emotions* ... the consequences of acting on your emotions instead of thinking things through, can be life-altering ... or even life-ending. And unfortunately, those consequences can never, ever be taken back.

When we read that nearly one third of the births in this country today occur outside of marriage, it's a stern reminder that decisions based on emotions can have consequences that live on long after we have died! That's why today, in an age where people have more freedom ... more temptations ... more distractions ... and more permissiveness than ever before in history, it's crucial that people fully understand and respect the power of their emotions and learn to manage them.

Use Your Head, Not Your Heart

A wise man once remarked, "Half our mistakes in life arise from feeling where we ought to think ... and thinking where we ought to feel." Every day we hear about, or observe, the truth of that statement.

> *"Half our mistakes in life arise from feeling where we ought to think ... and thinking where we ought to feel."*
>
> —Anonymous

For example, have you ever known anybody at work who quit his job in a fit of anger ... only to regret his decision the next day?

Have you ever observed a grossly overweight person order a huge, calorie-drenched meal and then say to the waiter, "And I'll have a diet Coke — I'm watching my weight"?

Have you ever known friends who bought a new car on impulse, even though they were maxed out on their credit cards and were living from paycheck to paycheck?

Have you ever known people who passed up an opportunity of a lifetime because they were afraid they might fail?

These are examples of people who failed to effectively manage their emotions.

My major in college was criminal justice, and, as part of my graduation requirements, I visited several of the state prisons and worked as an intern at the Public Defender's office. I can tell you from firsthand experience that our prisons would not be so full today if the inmates had learned to manage their emotions!

God Wants Us to Feel, Or He Wouldn't Have Given Us Emotions in the First Place

Now, don't think for a minute that I'm suggesting that emotions are bad. To the contrary, emotions are a big part of life!

Can you imagine living in a world where you couldn't feel love?
Can you imagine living in a world where you couldn't feel passion?
Can you imagine living in a world where you couldn't feel pride?

Can you imagine living in a world where you couldn't feel enthusiasm ... or joy?

Nor am I suggesting that you should go around holding your emotions inside, like a human pressure cooker just waiting to explode. All the medical research indicates that people who don't have a proper outlet for their emotions are most at risk for heart attacks, strokes, ulcers and a whole host of other problems.

It's okay to feel all your emotions, even the ones that we don't like to acknowledge, like jealousy ... and envy ... and, yes, even anger. And under the right circumstances, it's okay to vent those emotions.

Even the Bible doesn't exhort us to deny our feelings, much less to suppress them. God wants us to feel the full range of emotions that He granted us, or He wouldn't have given those emotions to us in the first place! There's even a place for feeling hate, for God commands us to *"love the sinner, but hate the sin."*

Even though the Bible is full of stories about people who are punished for letting their emotions get the best of them — as was the case in the story of Samson and Delilah, for example — the Bible also reminds us that there are occasions when it's perfectly appropriate to wear our emotions on our sleeve, just as Jesus did when he angrily drove the money-changers and the merchants out of the Temple in Jerusalem.

Make Your Emotions Work for You, Not Against You

As the Bible makes clear time after time, managing your emotions doesn't mean you stop feeling ... or even that you stop expressing yourself.

Managing your emotions means you don't overreact — or underreact, for that matter — to situations ...

Managing your emotions means you take a moment to put things in perspective ...

Managing your emotions means you remain firmly in control so that your emotions enhance your life, rather than ruin it.

Managing your emotions means making them work FOR you, not AGAINST you.

I'd like to share with you a true-life story about a talented athlete that illustrates how someone can turn their life around once they learn to manage their emotions.

Learning to Control His Emotions the Hard Way

When the athlete was only a boy, it was obvious to everybody that he was blessed with special physical gifts. He was much faster than the other boys his age, and his endurance, even as a youngster, was astonishing. He loved all sports, and excelled at every one he ever tried.

When he was nine years old, his father handed him a warped wooden tennis racquet and took him to the local park to hit some balls. From the first swing of the racquet, the boy was hooked! It wasn't long before he was beating all the kids in his hometown ... then all the kids his age throughout the country.

By the time he was 12, he was regularly beating the best adult players in his country, and he could give world-class tennis pros a run for their money. Everyone predicted he would be a world champion one day ... that is, if he only learned how to control his temper.

You see, the boy was so talented and competitive that he expected to win every point. And when something went wrong, like when he missed an easy shot ... or if an umpire made a bad call ... the boy had a fit.

When things didn't go his way, he'd curse ... he'd stop play and argue with the umpires ... he'd throw his racquet. On more than one occasion he smashed his racquet against the steel net posts until it was mangled and splintered. His temper got so out of control that he started complaining more than playing ... and he began losing matches he should have won.

One day his father came out to watch him in the finals of a big tournament. Sure enough, the boy started losing his temper .. shouting ... cursing ... throwing his racquet, the whole routine. After 10 minutes of witnessing this obnoxious behavior, the father had had enough.

He got up from his seat in the stands, walked onto the court during the middle of a point, and announced to everyone present, *"This match is over. My son defaults."* With that he walked over to his son, grabbed his racquet, and said in a stern voice, *"Come with me."*

No Tennis for Six Months

When they got home the father placed the racquet in a closet and said to his son in an even voice, *"This racquet will stay in this closet for six months. You are not to touch this racquet or any other racquet until the six months are up, end of discussion."*

The boy was crushed! Tennis was his life ... his passion. And it would be half a year before he could even hold a racquet. To a twelve-year-old boy, six months was like six years. How would he survive six months without tennis?

At the end of the six months, his father removed the racquet from the closet, and handed it to his son with these words: *"If I hear so much as one curse word pass your lips ... so much as one toss of your racquet in anger, I'll take it from you for good. Either you control your temper, or I will control it for you."*

The boy was so overjoyed to be able to play that he took to the sport with more passion than ever before. By the time he was 15, he was beating many of the touring pros. At 16, he was winning professional tournaments all over Europe.

From a Whiner to a Winner

With each tournament, the young man was getting better and better, and the press started calling him "teen angel," because he looked so young and innocent ... and because on the court, he behaved like an angel! You see, after his father's suspension, the boy learned to manage his emotions even under the most stressful conditions. Even if he was victimized by a terrible line call in the finals of a major tournament, he handled the situation with poise.

He became such a master at controlling his emotions, that his opponents became intimidated by his on-court demeanor. Whether it was the first point of an easy match ... or the last nerve-racking point of a hard-fought final, his expression and demeanor remained the same. He was in complete control of his emotions.

The young man went on to become what many experts consider the greatest player to ever pick up a tennis racquet. He won 14 major championships in all, including six French Open titles — the first when he was only 18 years old — and five straight Wimbledon titles. The one-time tennis brat ... later known as "Teen-Angel" ... was none other than Bjorn Borg.

Borg would be the first to admit that learning to manage his emotions was the turning point in his tennis career, if not his life. Because he learned to control his emotions, he transformed himself from a *whiner* who was always on the verge of self destruction ... to a *winner* who remained calm and cool even during the hottest moments of competition.

You Choose Your Emotions

Borg learned the hard way that it was up to him to keep his emotions under control. That's really what I'm talking about when I say you must manage your emotions. You have to control your emotions, or they will control you.

When my children were four and five years old, they would sometimes try to blame my wife ... or me ... when their anger got the best of them. *"You made me mad when you wouldn't let me ride my bike after dinner,"* Nathan used to shout at me when I'd reprimand him for stomping around the house when he didn't get his way. Or he'd shout, *"I threw the ball in the house because Burkie made me mad when he called me names."*

I take time to explain to all four of my kids that I'm not personally responsible for their emotions. No one made them mad or sad or happy or glad. Those are emotions they have chosen. Whether you are five years old or fifty-five years old, managing your emotions means understanding that you can't always control what happens to you ... But as Bjorn Borg learned, you CAN control your emotional response.

In order to discover the CEO within, it's imperative that you learn to manage your emotions. When people use phrases like, "He made a sound business decision" ... or "It has to make good business sense," what they're really saying is you have to think with your head, not your heart.

Three Powerful Emotions

What I'd like to do in the rest of this chapter is to discuss three universal emotions that have the power to make or break YOU, INC. ... and to discuss how we can effectively manage these emotions so that they work *for us, not against us.* The emotions we're going to discuss are *Fear ... Worry ... and Enthusiasm.*

Managing Fear

Let's start with fear because it's perhaps the strongest emotion known to humans. Now, when I say fear, I'm not talking about the fear you'd feel if you were walking alone through Central Park at night. When I talk about fear, I mean fear of the unknown, or more precisely, fear of failure and fear of rejection.

So the question is, "How do you manage fear?"

The key to managing fear is to face it head on, not to put on a face of bravado and pretend fear doesn't exist. To be honest, we're all afraid from time to time. That's only human. The problem is that some people — too many people, actually — try to avoid fear by hiding from it. As a wise person once put it, *"A ship in harbor is safe. But that's not what ships are built for."*

Avoiding fear by "playing it safe," if there is such a thing ... or by refusing to take risks ... isn't managing fear. It's letting fear manage you because fear is calling the shots, not you. The best way to

. . . .

manage fear is to understand it ... and then to use it as a motivator instead of an inhibitor.

A good example of someone who often used fear as a motivator is the versatile actor Rex Harrison. You may remember him as Professor Higgins in the classic musical *My Fair Lady*.

After the filming of *My Fair Lady* was completed, the actors took a couple of weeks off before assembling to record the soundtrack for the album. On the appointed day, all the actors showed up at the recording studio wearing comfortable, everyday clothes. That is, everyone but Harrison.

> *"A ship in harbor is safe. But that's not what ships are built for."*
>
> *—Anonymous*

When Harrison arrived at the studio, everyone was amazed to see that he was in full makeup and wearing the costume he wore for the movie. The producer approached Harrison and said, *"Rex, perhaps there's been a mix-up. We are recording the songs in a sound studio today, not filming scenes from the movie."*

Harrison studied the producer before replying dryly, *"My dear fellow, I know we are recording, not filming, today. But you see, I wanted to give my best performance. And in order for me to be at my best, I have to be dressed ... I have to have on my makeup ... and I have to be scared."*

The point of the story is that even superstars experience fear from time to time, just like you and me. What separates the superstars from the also-rans is their ability to manage their fears. Rex Harrison, for example, didn't deny he was scared and nervous. Instead, he used his fear to prepare himself so that he would give the best performance he was capable of. Now that's what I call being in control of your emotions and managing them!

Use Fear as a Motivator to Prepare

I think most of us look at successful people — especially athletes and entertainers — and assume they're somehow immune to feeling the emotions we "mortals" feel. Nothing could be further from the truth.

Don't you think Jack Nicklaus' heart pounds when he stands over a four-foot putt to win the Masters? ... Don't you think Michael Jordan gets scared when he's standing at the free throw line with the game tied and no time on the clock? ... Don't you think Tom Hanks gets scared when he delivers an Oscar acceptance speech before a TV audience of a billion people?

You bet they feel the same kind of emotions that every human would feel in their situation. The big difference is, successful people manage their emotions and use them to enhance their performances.

Helen Hayes, often called the First Lady of American Theater, enjoyed a career that spanned 60 years. Even at the end of her career, she admitted to getting butterflies before a performance. *"Of course I get scared up there,"* she once told an interviewer. *"But I don't think of fear as a deterrent. I think of it as a kick in the rear to prepare."*

Playing It Safe Isn't the Answer

Managing the emotion of fear reminds me of the story about the backwoods farmer who was sitting on his front steps during planting season. A stranger stopped at the farmer's house to ask for a drink of water.

"How's the wheat coming along?" asked the stranger.

"Didn't plant none," replied the farmer.

"Really?" said the stranger. *"I thought this was good wheat country."*

"I was afraid it wouldn't rain," said the farmer.

"Oh, well, how's the corn crop?" asked the stranger.

"Ain't got none," said the farmer.

"You didn't plant any corn either?" asked the puzzled stranger.

"Nope," said the farmer. *"Afraid of corn blight."*

"For heaven's sake," shouted the stranger, *"what did you plant?"*

"*Nothin'!*" said the farmer. "*I just played it safe.*"

Now I ask you, if we do indeed "reap what we sow," what will the farmer sow by playing it safe? That's right — absolutely nothing!

Managing Worry

The same could be said for managing the second emotion that is critical to YOU, INC. — worry. Like the farmer who played it safe, if you let your worries dominate your life, you'll end up far less productive than if you just tucked your worries in your back pocket and went for it.

One of the co-founders of the world-famous Mayo Clinic, Dr. Charles Mayo, had this to say about the negative effects of worry:

"*Worry affects circulation, the glands, the whole nervous system, and profoundly affects the heart. I have never known a man who died from overwork, but many who died from doubt.*"

> "I have never known a man who died from overwork, but many who died from doubt."
>
> — Dr. Charles Mayo

Isn't that a powerful statement? *I have never known a man who died from overwork, but many who died from doubt.* And it's especially appropriate for our times, a period in history that many economists are calling "The Age of Anxiety."

The problem with worry is it's such a waste of valuable time. Worry is like a rocking chair. It gives you something to do, but it doesn't get you anywhere. The best way I know to manage worry is to get out of your rocker and go DO something productive! Like fear, you can use worry as a kick in the pants to get you motivated to act, instead of allowing it to paralyze you.

Worrying Won't Pay the Bills

If you're worried about something, it's a good indication that you need to become proactive. There are millions of people in this country worried about losing their jobs. But worrying about it won't keep the pink slip out of their mailbox ... or the bill collector away from their door if and when it happens. Doesn't it make sense to manage worry by using it as a motivator to improve yourself so that you're more valuable to your employer ... or your business?

If you're worried about losing your job, maybe it's time to take a class to upgrade your skills ... to go back to school ... to seek out a mentor ... to network with your friends ... to explore what's available in other career areas. Be *productive*, instead of *reactive*.

If you choose to sit in the rocking chair of worry, all you will do is wear a hole in your carpet ... which means you'll have to worry about how you're going to find the money to pay to get the rug repaired!

People who worry all the time are like the story about the Chinese widow whose sole means of support was her two sons. The older son sold umbrellas. The younger son sold sunglasses. The old woman worried every single day, because when it was sunny, the older son wouldn't sell any umbrellas. If it were raining, the younger son wouldn't sell any sunglasses. So no matter what the weather, she worried ... and worried ... and worried.

One day a wise, old friend dropped by for a visit. The friend was alarmed at how thin and pale the widow had become. *"Are you ill, my dear friend?"* asked the woman. *"No, replied the widow. I'm just worried all the time. No matter what the weather, one of my sons will not make any sales for the day."*

The wise old friend smiled and said, *"Oh, no, my friend. You, of all people, shouldn't have a worry in the world, for you can't help but win. For you see, no matter what the weather, one of your sons will always sell his wares."*

How many times have you worried about something, only to find out that everything turned out fine in the end? What did that worry get you but headaches ... and lost sleep? Worry, my friend, is nothing more than the misuse of your imagination. All you have to do to manage your worry is to manage your imagination!

Are You Suffering from a Lack of Enthusiasm?

The last emotion that I want to discuss with you is one near and dear to my heart because I see it lacking in so many lives. What I'm talking about is enthusiasm ... or more to the point, *lack of enthusiasm!*

> *"The first fire we light is the one within."*
>
> — slogan for Campfire Girls & Boys

Lack of enthusiasm reminds me of the remark by an old politician when informed that his rival, President Calvin Coolidge, had died. The politician pondered for a moment before asking with a wry smile, *"Cal died, eh? How could they tell?"*

Sadly, there are a lot of people for whom that line would be appropriate. Too many of us get so caught up in our routines ... and bogged down with worries ... that we fail to stop and smell the roses. We get so distracted by the details of living that we lose that spark, that enthusiasm for life.

Genuine enthusiasm isn't something you put on or take off.

Genuine enthusiasm is a way of life!

The Origin of the Word "Enthusiasm"

The derivation of the word enthusiasm says it all. Enthusiasm comes from the Greek prefix *en*, meaning "within," and the word *theos*, which means "God." Put them together and you have a brilliant definition of enthusiasm: *en-theos*, or *God within*.

Think about it, if you have *God within*, you're radiant ... alive ... passionate ... powerful ... living ... real ... involved ... The list is endless!

That's why I love the slogan for the Campfire Girls and Boys. Their slogan says this: *"The first fire we light is the one within."* Isn't that great? The first priority of the Campfire Girls and Boys is to get those kids fired up and excited about life again. Now, that's a mission I can get behind in a big way!

I mean, if you don't have a fire within ... if you aren't excited about your life ... if you aren't excited about your work ... if you aren't excited about your family ... and if you aren't excited about your future — how do you expect anyone else to be excited about your life, your work, your family and your future?

The great American philosopher Emerson once said, *"Nothing great was ever achieved without enthusiasm."* Enthusiasm and success are like Siamese twins — it's hard to find one without the other!

> *"Nothing great was ever achieved without enthusiasm."*
>
> — *Ralph Waldo Emerson*

Look at it this way. Everyone is enthusiastic about something in their lives, isn't that true? The key to living a life of passion and vitality, then, is to capture your last feeling of enthusiasm and then extend it from 6 minutes ... to 60 minutes ... to 60 days ... to 60 months ... to 60 years!

To Be Alive Is to Be Enthusiastic

Let me close with a quote from one of the most passionate, enthusiastic, bombastic people I know of — Mel Brooks, the writer and producer of silly, off-the-wall movies like *Blazing Saddles* and *Young Frankenstein.* Here is what Brooks has to say about why it's so crucial that people cultivate the emotion of enthusiam in their lives:

"Look, I really don't want to wax philosophic, but I will say that if you're alive, you've got to flap your arms and legs. You've got to jump around a lot. You've got to make a lot of noise, because life is the very opposite of death.

"Therefore, as I see it, if you're quiet, you're not living. You've got to be noisy — or at least your thoughts should be noisy and colorful and lively so that no one will mistake you for dead before your time."

I look at it this way. I figure that Alexander Pope was right on the money when he wrote, *"The ruling passion, be what it will ... The ruling passion conquers reason still ..."*

It stands to reason that if I'm going to be ruled by a passion, then

. . . .

I'd much rather be ruled by enthusiasm than 99 percent of the other passions that are fighting to control my life.

So here's my advice to you: If you're going to give in to an emotion, give in to enthusiasm! And always remember ... it's never too late to take the advice of the Campfire Girls and Boys:

"The first fire you should light ... is the one within."

• • •

PRINCIPLE 8: _____
Prepare for Success

You hit home runs not by chance, but by preparation.
— Roger Maris

I'd like to open our discussion of Principle Number Eight, *Prepare for Success*, with a story about a famous episode in modern history that vividly illustrates the difference between *preparing yourself for success ... and preparing yourself for failure.*

The incident occurred on April 15, 1912, in the icy waters of the North Atlantic, when a British ocean liner on its maiden voyage smashed into a submerged iceberg.

The Tragedy of the *Titanic*

Ironically, the owners of the super ship, christened the *Titanic*, billed their vessel as the world's first unsinkable ship, by virtue of its double hull construction. The engineers of the *Titanic* theorized that in the event an underwater object ... like an iceberg ... pierced the outer hull, the ship would still float because the inner hull would remain intact.

The owners were so confident of their state-of-the-art engineering that they weren't prepared for what would happen if an iceberg pierced not only the first hull ... but the second hull, as well. Which is exactly what happened on that fateful night in 1912.

Tragically, the lack of preparation not only failed to prevent one of the worst peacetime disasters in the 20th century ... the *lack of preparation actually CAUSED the disaster!!*

Here are the seldom-discussed circumstances that led to the drowning of all but 700 of the passengers and crew members aboard the *Titanic's* maiden voyage:

Shortage of Lifeboats

Of the 1,500 men, women and children who drowned in the freezing arctic waters that night, how many do you think died because the ship hit an iceberg? The astonishing answer is ... *only a few!* The sad truth is the vast majority of the victims died because *the* Titanic *didn't have enough lifeboats!*

Unforgivable, isn't it, to think that a major catastrophe could have been avoided if only someone had *prepared* the *Titanic* for the unexpected, including how to save the passsengers in the unlikely event the world's first unsinkable ship did, in fact, sink. Even though the sinking of the *Titanic* occurred almost a century ago, it still stands as a timeless reminder of what can happen when we do NOT prepare properly.

Are You Preparing Yourself for Success — Or Failure?

The reason I'm sharing this story with you is because it serves as an appropriate metaphor for YOU, INC. You see, depending on how you are approaching your life and managing your time, you are either preparing yourself for success ... or you are preparing yourself for failure.

> *"The will to win is important. But the will to win isn't worth a nickel unless you also have THE WILL TO PREPARE!"*
>
> *— Rick Pitino*

Now, I truly believe the American people have the will to succeed. I don't doubt that for a moment. For the most part, Americans are ambitious ... resourceful ... creative ... and hard working. That's why we're the leader of the free world.

But I think the real reason more Americans aren't successful is NOT because we don't want to be successful. We do. The real reason more Americans aren't successful is because *not enough of us are properly preparing ourselves for success!*

Rick Pitino, coach of the University of Kentucky basketball team that won the 1996 NCAA championship, said it best:

"I'm not one of those guys who believes that the key to winning is the will to win. Don't kid yourself, the will to win is important. But the will to win isn't worth a nickel unless you also have THE WILL TO PREPARE!"

Obviously, Pitino's championship team had the will to prepare, because they steamrolled over the other teams in the tournament, winning by the record-setting margin of 17 points per game!

Now, consider this: If Rick Pitino had NOT prepared HIS TEAM for success, do you think Kentucky would have won the NCAA championship?

If Rick Pitino had NOT prepared *HIMSELF* for success, do you think he would be earning upward of a million dollars a year, with half a dozen NBA owners lined up to pay him double ... or even triple that amount? Not a chance!

The single biggest reason Rick Pitino is one of the most successful, highly paid and sought-after coaches in America is because of his legendary commitment to preparation.

Success Is Not an Accident

Think about this for a moment: When Pitino was a young assistant coach learning the ropes, he was earning less in a year than what he would get today for delivering a one-hour keynote speech! In other words, *by preparing for success,* Pitino has increased his value so dramatically that *one hour* of his time today is worth what *one year* of his time was worth 10 years ago! That's the power of preparation!

Here's my point: Success is not an accident. Successful people don't just stumble over a pot of gold while they are out walking the dog. Successful people, like the Rick Pitino's of the world, spend countless hours getting the knowledge and acquiring the skills that will increase the value of their services.

In America, Information Is Everywhere

Now, I'd be the first one to tell you that it's relatively easy to prepare yourself for success in America, as compared to most other countries. We have free public education here ... we have libraries in virtually every neighborhood ... we have hundreds of four-year colleges and scores of community colleges all over the country. I contend that anyone who is *serious* about getting the information that will help them prepare for success can get it.

> *"The more*
> *you learn ...*
> *the more*
> *you earn."*
>
> *— Harvey McKay*

You can't say that for Ecuador, where I grew up. In some parts of South America, children don't even have access to schools, much less libraries .... or trade schools ... or colleges. In South America, the vast majority of people don't have access to the information that could prepare them for prosperity and success. As a result, only the privileged few are afforded the opportunity to learn and grow. Fortunately, that's just not the case in America.

With all the vast resources available to us in America, I'm convinced that the key to preparation is personal initiative. Information and knowledge are readily available in this country, but you have to take the personal initiative to find it. You have to take the personal initiative to learn the skills you'll need to succeed.

Just look at the last six presidents of the United States. All but one came from middle class backgrounds, and two of our recent presidents, Ronald Reagan and Bill Clinton, grew up poor with abusive, alcoholic fathers. Say what you will about their politics, you can't deny that these men did what they had to do to prepare themselves for success.

The More You Learn ... The More You Earn!

So, the question becomes, where do we go? ... and what do we do to prepare ourselves for success? The answer is right in front of you: You've got to get the information and learn the skills by reading the books ... by attending the seminars ... by listening to the audios ... by taking the classes ... by taking the notes ... by doing the homework ... by subscribing to the publications ... by associating with the winners ... by visiting the library ... by heeding the weekly sermons ... and by learning from your mentors. That's how you get better prepared.

Increased preparation equals increased value. It's that simple. A perfect illustration can be seen in the field of medicine.

Why is a specialist more valuable than a general practitioner?

Why is a general practitioner more valuable than a registered nurse?

Why is a registered nurse more valuable than a nurse's aid?

The answer can be found in this simple equation: The better prepared you are, the more valuable you are. And the more valuable you are, the more you'll earn. Like Harvey McKay, the author of the *Swim with the Sharks Without Being Eaten Alive,* says: *The more you LEARN ... the more you EARN!*

Increased Knowledge Equals Increased Value

Think of it this way: If you had to undergo major surgery ... and you had to pay for the operation out of your own pocket ... who would you want performing the surgery — a world-renowned specialist ... or a young doctor fresh out of medical school? Assuming the specialist would charge *10 times more* than the doctor who just graduated, would the specialist be worth the extra money? You better believe it!

I can't over-emphasize the crucial importance of preparation! As I said earlier, in a free-market society like America, what you earn is directly proportional to what you learn. Let me repeat that one more time just so you won't forget it: *What you earn is directly proportional to what you learn.*

Rick Pitino didn't dramatically increase his value and become a multi-million-dollar-per-year man by winging it ... or by wishing for it! You'll never catch Rick Pitino resting on his laurels and winging it.

For that matter, you'll never catch any successful coach ... or successful athlete ... or successful business person ... or successful musician ... or successful auto mechanic ... or successful professional ... winging it. Plain and simple, successful people understand the importance of preparation!

Homework Never Ends

Tom Peters, the author of *In Search of Excellence*, one of the best-selling business books in history, tells a story about the first time he realized that preparation for success is a never-ending process. When Peters was 17 years old, his girlfriend invited him over to her home for dinner. The girl's father was a very successful surgeon, and they lived in a magnificent home on Cape Cod overlooking the ocean.

After dinner, while the rest of the family gathered in the living room to talk, the father excused himself and adjourned to the den, where he spent the rest of the evening reading medical journals and reviewing surgical procedures for an operation scheduled for the next morning.

> *"General knowledge, no matter how great in quantity or variety it may be, is of little use in the accumulation of money."*
>
> *— Napoleon Hill*

Up until this incident, Peters assumed that you went to school to get filled up with all the knowledge you'd need to do what you were going to do ... and then once you had all this knowledge, you wouldn't have to mess with studying and homework ever again.

But here Peters was in the home of a fabulously successful surgeon, a man who had spent four years in high school ... four years in college ... three years in medical school ... three more years as an intern ... and the man was still doing homework! *"It just didn't seem fair,"* Peters later mused, *"that homework would never end."*

Well, if you're serious about achieving success today, you're going to have to "do your homework," as Peters calls it, on an ongoing basis — you're going to have to commit to continuous preparation as a way of life!

What We Learn in School

Let's take a moment to talk about formal schooling and what it can — and cannot do — to help you prepare for success. I want to go on record as saying I'm a big proponent of formal education.

Can you imagine trying to learn how to read and write and perform basic math on your own? Only the rare genius can be expected to do something like that. Thank God America has free public education so that virtually every citizen can learn the basics, or what the old timers call "the three Rs" — readin', writin' and 'rithmatic!

As I see it, the main purpose of our early education is to teach us general knowledge. Now, let me make this clear — general knowledge plays a crucial part in preparing each of us for success. General knowledge provides us with the basics so we can continue our preparation. But make no mistake, general knowledge is NOT an end in itself!

In Napoleon Hill's words, and I quote: *"General knowledge, no matter how great in quantity or variety it may be, is of little use in the accumulation of money."*

Specialized Knowledge Is the Key to Success

The key to success is *specialized* knowledge. Specialized knowledge is where the real preparation for success takes place — this is where we can dramatically increase our fair market value.

Colleges are certainly one place where people can acquire specialized knowledge, like graduating with a degree in accounting. Graduate schools, medical schools and law schools are other formal methods for acquiring specialized knowledge.

Unfortunately, too many of us think of graduation as an *end* to our education ... when in fact, graduation isn't the end — *it's the beginning!* That's why we attend *commencement* ceremonies to receive our diplomas. To *commence* means to begin or to start.

The purpose of the commencement ceremony is NOT to *celebrate the end of our education.* The purpose of the commencement ceremony is to tell us we're finally free to *commence our real education.*

Certainly, traditional education is important. But if you had a list of all the successful people, in and by itself, who dropped out of school, you'd soon realize that formal education isn't the key to preparing for success.

There's No Substitute for Personal Initiative

Bill Gates, the richest man in America, is a college drop-out.

So is Wayne Huizenga, the founder of Blockbuster Video.

Henry Ford never made it through high school.

And Thomas Edison only got to the fourth grade! The difference between most drop-outs and these super-successful men is their level of commitment to life-long learning.

The Bill Gates' and the Wayne Huizenga's of the world understand that the only way to dramatically increase the value of YOU, INC., is through personal initiative. Gates didn't learn to design software sitting in a classroom. Gates learned about software by reading IBM software manuals and picking the brains of the programmers.

Gates knew instinctively that in order to prepare for success, YOU have to take the initiative to get the knowledge ... YOU have to take the initiative to acquire the skills ... YOU have take the initiative to polish your strengths until they outshine your competitor's ... and YOU have to take the initiative to improve on your weaknesses so that they don't become your downfall.

So, the obvious question is, where do you get the information that will increase your fair market value? Where do you find the knowledge? Where do you learn the skills?

The Best Sources of Information

Earlier in this section I listed all the places where you can get the preparation you need to succeed. What I'd like to do now is to identify what I consider the four best sources to gain knowledge and understanding, and then to discuss each of these sources in a little detail. Here they are, in no particular order:

One, *books;*

two, *tapes;*
three, *seminars;*
and four, *relationships.*

Let's start by discussing how you can dramatically increase your value by reading on a daily basis.

Read 10 Pages a Day

Do you think you could make the time to read 10 pages of a book every day? For most people, that would mean setting aside 20 to 30 minutes each and every day to read. If you would read 10 pages a day, do you know how many 180-page books you could read in a year's time? The answer is almost 20 books!

Over the course of 10 years, that would calculate to be approximately 200 books. Now, do you think it's fair to say that you could add significant value to YOU, INC. if you read 200 quality books on a wide range of topics? Obviously!

There are a lot of great books available that can help you prepare for success. *Read a book on time management.* You need to know where to spend your time to the get the most out of each day.

Read a book on self-motivation. We all get down from time to time, so we've got to feed our minds with positive information that can get us out of the doldrums and back on track.

Read a book about how to become a better parent. Read a book about the latest economic and business trends. Read a book of poetry. Read a book about a multi-millionaire. Read a book on each of the 10 principles we discuss in YOU, INC. Read ... read ... read!

The Readers vs. the Read-nots

We've all heard the politicians talk about the "*have's*" and the "*have not's,*" right? Well, according to a recent survey by the American Library Association, the "*have's*" — that is, the top 20 percent of the income earners in America — are reading more books than ever before. That's why book sales in this country have been going up every year!

The "have not's," however, aren't buying books. The "have not's" aren't even going to the library to check them out for free. The "have not's" have become the *"read not's"* ... and not because they CAN'T read. The vast majority of the "read not's" are CHOOSING NOT TO READ!

> *"The person who can read and doesn't is just as bad off as the person who can't read."*
>
> —*Anonymous*

Check this out: The percentage of illiterate Americans has stayed about the same since the 1960's. Yet a growing number of Americans who can read are choosing NOT to read — by some estimates, as much as 20 percent of literate Americans are "read not's." This is simply inexcusable!

A wise person once said, *"The person who can read and doesn't is just as bad off as the person who can't read."* I'll go one step further. The person who can read but doesn't is WORSE off than the person who can't because they are choosing to let a valuable skill go to waste! That's a shame!

Correlation Between Not Reading and Not Having

Do you think there's a correlation, here, between *not having* and *not reading?* You bet there is! And in a country like ours, with a bookstore on virtually every corner ... with a branch library in virtually every neighborhood ... with information on the World Wide Web virtually at our fingertips ... it's a national disgrace for literate people to avoid reading!

There's simply no excuse for being ignorant in America. NONE!

Audio and Video Tapes

Now let's look at another terrific source for acquiring knowledge and information — audio and video tapes. Audio and video tapes are great sources of information because they're affordable and convenient.

With video tapes, you can attend a professional seminar on

virtually any topic in the comfort of your living room; with audio tapes, you can receive a first-class education while driving to and from work.

Remember now, it wasn't that many years ago in this country that people had to go to extraordinary lengths to get an education. We've all heard stories from our parents or grandparents about the "olden" days when they had to walk five miles to and from school. Or the stories about Abraham Lincoln fashioning a homemade chalkboard and then writing out his school lessons by the light of the fireplace.

We're not talking Hollywood fiction, here. We're only a couple of generations removed from the one-room schoolhouse. But look how easy it is to access information today. The fact is, technology has brought the school right to our doorstep, so to speak.

It's so easy to get information today that it's like falling off a log! Audio and video tapes are so readily accessible and available today that it's inexcusable NOT to increase your knowledge on a daily basis.

Think of it this way. What would you pay to have the world's best thinkers ... the wealthiest business people ... the wisest philosophers ... the most respected experts in the field of your choice — ride with you in your car every day giving you their sage advice?

Your Car Can Be a Classroom on Wheels

Would you pay a $100 an hour to spend the afternoon riding around with Zig Ziglar, one of the greatest sales trainers and motivators in the world?

Would it be worth $1,000 to you to commute to and from work for a week with Warren Buffett, the billionaire investor?

Well, with audio tapes, you can pick the brains of the Ziglar's and Buffett's of the world for literally pennies a day. What intelligent person who wants more out of life would NOT jump at the chance to turn an unproductive commute into an information-filled educational experience?

Do you have any idea how much General Motors invests every year in research and development? *GM spends more than one billion dollars every year on R&D!* A billion dollars each and every year!

Do you think that might be a major reason GM is one of the most profitable companies in the world! You bet it is!

What's Your R&D Budget for YOU, INC.?

Let's say you invested $100 a month on books and tapes to improve YOU, INC. That's $1,200 a year, right? And to many people, that's a lot of money. But would it be worth it for you to invest $25 a week on improving YOU, INC. if you knew it could dramatically increase your fair market value? Would you spend, for example, $1,000 a year for information that would help you earn an extra $10,000 — or maybe even an extra $100,000 — a year? Wouldn't that be a wise investment of your time and money? I hope to shout!

> *"It's what
> you learn after
> you know it all
> that counts."*
>
> *— John Wooden*

The truth of the matter is this: If you're NOT investing a portion of your gross income toward the R&D of YOU, INC., you're setting yourself up for failure. Like John Wooden, the most successful coach in the history of college basketball, says: *"It's what you learn after you know it all that counts."*

Educational Seminars and Training Events

Third on my list of key sources for acquiring knowledge is live seminars or events. Not a week goes by that I don't get a fistful of flyers in the mail promoting seminars on a full range of topics — everything from "how to manage your time more effectively" to "improving your communication skills." I'll bet you could attend a local seminar that would improve YOU, INC. virtually every week of the year!

Full Serving of the "-TIONS"

What I really like about attending live seminars is that you get a full serving of what I call the "T-I-O-N-S." The "-tions" I'm talking about are informa-*tion* ... educa-*tion* ... inspira-*tion* ... emo-*tion* ... motiva-*tion* ... interac-*tion* ... and valida-*tion*.

Do you think attending a seminar that teaches you how to better communicate with your spouse could improve your marriage?

Do you think a seminar that explains painless ways to save money could help you prepare for a more secure retirement?

Do you think that a seminar that teaches you proven methods for increasing your income could improve your lifestyle? Obviously!

A worthwhile seminar is, in effect, a highly specific graduate course condensed into a few days or a few hours. If you consider what books and tuition for one college class costs today, you'd have to agree that most seminars are a bargain!

Relationships

The final source of information and knowledge I want to discuss with you is relationships. Like my mom always says, *"Tell me who you hang out with, and I'll tell you who you are."*

If you hang out with people who read books ... listen to tapes ... and attend seminars, guess what? There's a good chance you'll read books ... listen to tapes ... and attend seminars! This isn't rocket science here, folks. This is just good old common sense!

You hang out with eagles, and guess what, you start acting like an eagle. You start flying like an eagle. But can you guess what happens to people who hang out with ducks? That's right .... they start to quack and walk like a duck. Have you ever heard the expression "he's a sitting duck"? It means someone is just sitting there, waiting for disaster to strike!

When preparing yourself for success, you must seek out life long relationships with winners who are excited and have a purpose ... instead of associating with losers who get jealous when you start doing better than they are.

To prepare yourself for success, you have to cultivate honest relationships with mentors who can help you reach a new level of achievement. To prepare yourself for success, you have to forge new relationships with people who will challenge you to grow and break out of your comfort zone. To prepare yourself for success, you must let go of the people who are holding you back.

The Power of a Partnership

Allow me to illustrate the power of relationships with a story about three young boys walking down the railroad tracks.

One of the boys was a much better athlete than the other two, and he was always challenging them to a contest, which he invariably won.

About a mile outside town, the athletic boy challenged the other two boys to see who could walk the farthest on the rails. *"I'll go first,"* the athletic boy shouted with a confident smile. He jumped on one of the rails and walked almost 100 yards before losing his balance. *"Beat that,"* he crowed to the other two boys.

The two less coordinated boys knew they couldn't outdo their athletic friend by themselves, so they huddled briefly and devised an ingenious plan: With the help of his friend, one boy balanced himself on a rail. The other boy walked to the opposite rail and — without letting go of his friend's hand — carefully balanced himself on the rail. Then, still holding hands, the two friends walked side by side on the rails ... all the way into town!

What a terrific illustration of how a relationship between two people with a specific purpose can produce much greater results than if each person operated individually!

No Excuses for Lack of Preparation

I want to close this section with a story about a woman who truly understands what it means to prepare for success. The woman's name is Laura Sloate, and she is the senior partner of a New York money-management firm that oversees half a billion dollars in assets.

Sloate is phenomenally successful, by the way. During one five-year span, the private accounts she managed averaged returns of 25 percent or more a year!

Needless to say, in Sloate's line of work, her job is information intensive. She has to constantly monitor international markets ... she must assess scores of financial reports every week ... and she must stay on top of even the smallest global buying trends.

Sloate's success comes as no surprise to people who know her, for, according to her friends and family, she has been preparing herself for success ever since she was a little girl.

Even as a child Sloate listened to tapes ... attended seminars ... and counseled with mentors. Since age six she has sought out every piece of new technology that could help her prepare herself for success. Amazingly, the only thing she did not do ... was read.

In fact, to this day, Laura Sloate does not read, despite the fact that information is the life blood of her business. That's not to say that Laura Sloate is undisciplined. Or unprepared. To the contrary, Laura Sloate is a fountain of information on just about any subject you can think of. But as unlikely as it may seem, she didn't get that information through reading.

You see — *Laura Sloate has been blind since age six!*

> *"You can make excuses ... or you can make money. But you can't make them both at the same time!"*
>
> *—Anonymous*

If Laura Sloate Can Prepare for Success, So Can You!

There are two great lessons we can learn form Laura Sloate: First, her story reminds us that in the Information Age, we've got to do our homework. We can't rest on our laurels. Like Laura Sloate, we've got to keep on top of information every single day ... we've got to sharpen the old skills and learn new ones or we'll be left out in the cold.

And the second lesson Laura Sloate's remarkable story teaches us is that we can't make excuses for NOT preparing ourselves for success. People tell me all the time that they're just so bone-tired at the end of the day they can't possibly read 10 pages a night.

Others complain that they're so busy they can't possibly attend weekend seminars to learn a new skill.

Still others bemoan the fact that they're on such a tight budget they can't possibly afford to buy self-improvement books and motivational tapes.

Well, I believe that you can't afford NOT to buy them! Like I said before, *"You can make excuses ... or you can make money. But you can't make them both at the same time!"*

No Excuses

All I know is Laura Sloate has a better excuse than 99 percent of the people in this world, and it didn't stop her from preparing for success. All I know is Laura Sloate calls her blindness a "non-issue" that she and her employees never even think about. All I know is if Laura Sloate can prepare herself for success, SO CAN YOU!

The long and short of it is Laura Sloate chose to *prepare herself for success* ... rather than choosing to use her limitations as an excuse to *prepare herself for failure.*

Likewise, you and I have a choice. We can choose NOT to prepare ourselves for success — and end up a disaster, like the *Titanic.* Or we can choose to prepare ourselves for success — and end up like Laura Sloate.

As for me, I have chosen to sail with the Laura Sloate's of the world. HOW ABOUT YOU?

. . .

PRINCIPLE 9:
Balance Your Life

When the One Great Scorer
Comes to write against your name;
He marks, not that you won or lost,
But how you played the game.

— Grantland Rice

America is a country out of balance. All you have to do is scan any edition of your local newspaper for proof. Here's what you'll read:

- Bankruptcies are up.
- Incomes are down.
- One third of all babies are born out of wedlock.
- One third of Americans are overweight.
- Half of the marriages in this country end in divorce.
- Prisons are overcrowded.
- Children are out of control.
- Church attendance is spiraling downward.

More Out Than In

Statistics show that more and more Americans are suffering from a bad case of the *outs* — as in, *zoned out mentally ... tuned out spiritually ... tapped out financially ... and stressed out physically.* It seems like we're more OUT than IN these days.

When we're out of balance, we're listing to one side or the other, just waiting for a strong wind or a big wave to capsize us. But when we're in balance, we're solid ... we're stable ... we're upright ... and we're more likely to remain that way, no matter what the weather conditions.

Out of Balance ... Out of Control

People whose lives are out of balance are disasters waiting to happen. Just look at what happens to so many famous people who "have it all," so to speak ... only to *lose it all* when their lives veer out of balance.

Elvis Presley, the singer who sold more records than anyone in history, died at age 42, disoriented by drugs and 70 pounds overweight.

Marilyn Monroe, the most beautiful woman in the world, died before her 40th birthday from an apparent suicide brought on by depression.

Ty Cobb, one of the greatest hitters in the history of baseball, often said he wished he'd had a few less hits and a few more friends. He died alone and friendless.

Joe Louis, the professional boxer who won millions of dollars during his 12-year reign as heavyweight champion of the world, spent his last decades flat broke, surviving off the charity of others.

I could fill up this entire section with examples of world-famous people who self-destructed because they lacked balance in their lives.

But before I go into a discussion of how to balance your life, let me share a brief story with you about a fascinating news clip I happened to see. The news clip covered the demonstration of an amazing new boat, and I saw immediately that the boat's unique design serves as a vivid reminder of the importance of balance.

Unsinkable Coast Guard Boat

Let me preface this story by telling you that I've had a lifelong love affair with boats. My family has always lived near the ocean, so I've either enjoyed boating or owned a boat since I was old enough to swim. I tell you this so that you'll better understand the dramatic impression this boat demonstration had on me — it just blew me away!

The demonstration featured a new rescue boat designed especially for the Coast Guard called the Heavy Weather Patrol and Rescue Boat.

The boat can withstand the worst ocean storms, for it is designed to right itself in less than six seconds when flipped over on its side. In fact, the Coast Guard says the boat can be flipped end over end — bow over stern, to use nautical terms — and still turn right side-up in 20 seconds!

The clip showed a test where the boat was pulled over on its back, so that the bottom of the hull pointed straight up in the air. Sure enough, the boat popped back up like a cork, and then motored away under its own power!

The key to the boat's amazing balance is a honeycombed combination of air chambers placed throughout the interior hull. As a result, pushing the boat underwater is like trying to push a basketball underwater. Just as the air in the basketball resists your pressure to push it underwater ... the air in the boat chambers forces the boat back to the surface.

Balance Helps Us Battle the Storms in Our Lives

There is, however, a downside to this buoyant boat. The air chambers take up so much room that the space aboard the boat is tight, leaving only enough room in the hull for a pilot house and a survivor's compartment. In the words of the builder, *"This is not a luxury yacht. You have to give up a lot to get buoyancy space."*

Now, there are several lessons we can learn from this amazing rescue vessel. First and foremost, of course, is the concept of balance. The boat is a perfect metaphor for the importance of balancing our lives. When we have balance in our lives, we have stability ... even when we are threatened by sudden, unpredictable storms.

> *"For what does a man profit, if he shall gain the whole world, and lose his own soul?"*
>
> — Matthew 16:26

The reality of life is that strong winds and sudden waves may knock us over on our sides without warning. We may even end up flat on our backs. But when we have balance in our lives, we are able to right ourselves quickly and keep moving toward our destination. That's why balance is so important. In fact, that's why balance is essential for our well-being.

You Have to Give Up Something to Get Something

The other part of this metaphor that is so apropos is what the builder had to say about the design: *"This is not a luxury yacht. You have to give up a lot to get buoyancy space."*

> *"My best friend is the one who brings out the best in me."*
>
> — Henry Ford

Think about the builder's statement for a moment: *"You have to give up a lot to get buoyancy space."* In other words, he's saying there's a trade-off. Like everything in life, you have to give up something to get something in return.

Getting balance back in your life is the same way. There's a trade-off. You can't have your cake and eat it, too, so to speak. You can't eat pizza every night of the week and wash it down with a gallon of ice cream and expect to stay thin and healthy. Getting the proper balance means you may have to give up some things because they make you list to one side ... and you may have to add some other things so that you stay upright in the water, even when the wind blows.

Immutable Law of the Universe

When you think about it, proper balance is essential to keeping virtually everything in the world running on a smooth course. Just look at some of the phrases that indicate the importance of balance:

When the "balance of power" among nations gets out of kilter, war is likely to break out.

When the "trade balance" between countries gets lopsided, trade barriers go up.

When the "balance of nature" gets thrown out of sync, plants and animals face extinction. Balance is an immutable law of the universe. And we violate that law at our own risk!

The Benefits of Balance

Now let's get to the core of the matter: What does it mean to get balance in our lives? Let me answer that question by asking you a question: Do you remember when you first learned how to ride a bike? What happened when you leaned too far to one side? You fell over, didn't you?

So the next time you compensated a bit too much to the other side and — crash, you fell again. Eventually, through trial and error ... and lots of practice ... and a couple of scraped knees, you learned, first, the *value* of balance ... and second, you learned *how* to keep your balance.

Lo and behold ... after you learned how to balance dead-center in the middle of your bike, you could ride for miles on end without ever falling!

> *"There are three things that are extremely hard: steel, a diamond, and to know one's self."*
>
> — Benjamin Franklin

Do you remember that feeling? Wasn't that a terrific accomplishment? You bet it was! And that's exactly what can happen when you get your life in balance.

You see, life is like riding a bicycle. If you're off balance in your life, you will fall — which means you won't be able to reach your destination ... and you certainly won't enjoy the journey!

Balance and YOU, INC.

You may be asking yourself, "What does all this talk about balance have to do with YOU, INC.?" My answer is ... "ONLY EVERYTHING!"

YOU, INC. is about dramatically improving your value in *all areas of your life*, not just your bank account. Like the Bible says, *"For what does a man profit, if he shall gain the whole world, and lose his own soul?*" In other words, money is not an end in itself. Money is a MEANS to an end ... and that end is to *add balance* to your life.

The Story of Silas Marner

Did you ever read the novel *Silas Marner* in high school? Silas Marner was a miserly hermit whose sole pleasure in life was going home and counting his money every night. At the opening of the novel he was financially rich, but his life was totally out of balance.

He was friendless ...

He was Godless ...

He was loveless.

But when an orphaned baby mysteriously turned up on his doorstep, it changed his life dramatically overnight by forcing Silas Marner to add balance to his life. In the process of adding balance to his YOU, INC., Silas Marner began to open his heart ... and mind ... to emotions and experiences he had neglected for years. By the end of the novel, Silas Marner was not only well off financially, but he was far richer in the other areas of his life.

That's what I mean when I talk about the need to balance your life. If you're neglecting some areas of your life — like your family and your friends — while concentrating on others too much — like trying to get rich — you're walking headlong into the Silas Marner trap.

Maintaining the Five Fs in Your Life

Now I'd like to discuss the five areas of your life that give you balance. I first heard these five areas desribed as the "Five F's" in a speech by Jim Hansberger, a very successful stockbroker.

The key to balancing your life is to allot equal amounts of time and attention to each of the Five F's. Here they are in the order of their importance.

One, *Faith.*

Two, *Family.*

Three, *Fitness.*

Four, *Friends*.

And five, *Finances*.

To better explain how the Five F's affect the balance in your life, I'd like for you to think of balance as a wheel. In the center of the wheel is a hub called Faith. The spokes connecting the hub to the rim of the wheel would be the other four F's — that is, *Family* ... *Fitness* ... *Friends* ... *and Finances*.

If the hub is weak or missing, the wheel will collapse under even the slightest pressure. If one or more of the spokes are weak or missing, the wheel gets wobbly and bent when it hits bumps and potholes in the road of life.

But when the hub is strong ... when the spokes are solid and spaced equally inside the wheel ... when the wheel is oiled and maintained on a regular basis ... it will serve our needs and endure a lifetime!

Now let's take a few moments to discuss each of the Five F's so that we fully understand — and appreciate — why each area is deserving of our time ... our talents ... our efforts ... and our commitment.

Faith

Let's begin our discussion with the first F on our list — the hub ... the center of our balance wheel — the concept of *Faith*. As a starting point, I want to remind you of an indisputable truth:

There is a Creator.

Just as a book is proof of an author ... just as a poem is proof of a poet ... just as a song is proof of a composer ... creation is proof of a creator.

As far as I'm concerned, scientists can theorize until the end of time that life is a cosmic accident caused by the "Big Bang." And philosophers can write volumes and volumes of books about why God is dead.

All I know is this. If it weren't for an infinitely intelligent ... and an infinitely loving Creator I call God, I wouldn't be here to write this ... and you wouldn't be here to read it.

The best-selling book of all time — the Bible (and, I might add, the Bible has led the best-seller list every year since the list was formed) — defines faith as *"the substance of things hoped for, the evidence of things not seen."*

Just because you can't see faith, does that mean it doesn't exist? Does that mean it isn't real? Of course not! In fact, more and more scientific research proves that faith is alive ... and as real as real can be!

The Healing Power of Faith

Dr. Larry Dossey, former chief of staff at Medical City Dallas Hospital, wrote a book called, *Healing Words: The Power of Prayer and the Practice of Medicine.* In his book, Dr. Dossey cites 130 studies over the past 30 years that overwhelmingly prove that faith manifested through the power of prayer can help patients heal.

Dossey calls prayer, "... one of the best-kept secrets in medical science." Dossey sums up his findings with these words: *"When people enter into a prayerful state of mind, good things happen to those they pray for."*

No Atheists in a Foxhole

There's an old saying that you won't find any atheists in a foxhole during a war. That's a clever way of saying that in times of need, we always turn to God.

No question that God is a source of strength and hope in our times of need. But people who wait until they are on their deathbeds to bargain with God aren't living with faith as the center of their lives. And that's their loss. As a wise man once said, *"A man who does not pray can know a lot about God. But only a man who prays can KNOW God."* Knowing God through faith and prayer, then, is the first area that we need to focus on to balance our lives.

Family

The second F of the Five F's is *Family.* As the father of four children, I can tell you firsthand the importance of family. I still live within 20 minutes of my mother and step-father, and I talk to them just about every single day.

I'm often amazed at the number of people I meet who aren't close to their families. Seems like in our mobile society, it's the rule — rather than the exception — for children to live thousands of miles from their parents. If that's not bad enough, lots of my friends and acquaintances don't even talk to their parents once a week — much less visit them.

All too many people phone their parents less than once a month — and then don't make it a point to honor them by sending cards and gifts on special days, like birthdays ... Mother's Day ... Father's Day ... and the like.

Think about it — your parents laid the foundation of everything you are or will become! Short of your parents being criminal or abusive, you owe them not only your love, but also your respect ... and your kindness.

> *"A man who does not pray can know a lot about God. But only a man who prays can KNOW God."*
>
> *—Anonymous*

It's tragic when people need to be reminded that a strong family is a key ingredient to a balanced life. That's like telling thirsty people that they should drink water. How obvious can you get?

The Greatest Form of Abuse Today

It's frustrating to see people taking their families for granted and ignoring them. Ignoring your children ... or ignoring your parents ... or ignoring your spouse ... is the single greatest form of abuse in the world today.

You don't have to be a child psychiatrist to figure out that many children misbehave just so someone will pay attention to them.

Neglected children would rather be punished with a spanking than be ignored. To them, negative attention is better than no attention at all! That's pretty sad, isn't it?

Ironically, we see more and more of this desperate behavior from kids every day! Let's wake people up, before it's too late! People must pay attention to their families or our society will never get back into balance!

My Family and Fidel Castro

I think the reason family is so important to me ... and why I never take my family for granted ... comes from the injustice dealt to my mom and dad at the hands of the communist tyrant, Fidel Castro.

You see, at one time my father was one of the wealthiest men in Cuba, worth more than $20 million. He woke up one morning in 1959 to discover that Castro had taken over all of his property and all of his businesses.

Growing up with parents who lost a sizable fortune taught me that money is important ... but that **FAMILY IS EVERYTHING!** My parents went from having live-in maids ... estates at the beach ... chauffeured limousines at their disposal day and night ... to having little more than each other. My dad and mom survived their fall from the penthouse to the basement because they had family to help cushion the blow.

Don't Take Your Family for Granted

Obviously, I get pretty passionate about the importance of family. You see, my father died when I was only 13 years old. Let me tell you, I'd love nothing more than to be able to sit with him by the pool and have a nice long talk. I'd love nothing more than to call him on the phone just to get his opinion on a business investment ... or to have him hear his granddaughter's first words.

But it won't happen. It can't happen. So when I hear about children who don't *make the time* to talk to their parents every chance they get, I feel sorry for them. People must learn to appreciate what they have!

If you haven't talked to your parents this week, take the time to call them! You don't have to have an occasion. Just call them and tell them you love and appreciate them. If you haven't taken your daughter or grandson to the park this week, do it! If you're fighting with a brother or sister, call and patch things up! There's no time like the present to start getting your family life back into balance ... before it's too late!

Fitness

Now let's discuss the third spoke in your balance wheel — Fitness. When I talk about fitness, I'm not necessarily talking about looking like Arnold Schwarzenegger if you're a man ... or an L.A. Lakers cheerleader if you're a woman. When I talk about fitness, I mean taking care of your body instead of abusing it.

Do you remember the TV advertisement for Geritol where the actor at the end of the commercial would look into the camera with a very somber expression and say, *"When you've got your health, you've got just about everything."*

Now, isn't that the absolute truth? *"When you've got your health, you've got just about everything."* Every time we get sick with the flu or a bad cold, it serves to remind us just how important it is to have good health. What's amazing is the number of Americans who consciously *choose* to jeopardize their health!

You Can Choose Good Health

It's one thing to get sick through no fault of your own, like coming down with the chicken pox or having your tonsils removed when you're a child.

But it's another thing for people to contract emphysema because they smoke cigarettes. Smokers didn't start out with bad lungs. Smokers made choices that *CAUSED* their lungs to malfunction.

People who abuse their bodies are not adding balance to their lives. They are sending out personal invitations to sickness and poor health. They are voluntarily, purposely throwing their health — and their lives — out of balance. And frankly, there's no excuse for that!

U.S.A. Today published a shocking graph a while back. The graph is proof that most Americans are choosing to make themselves sick, instead of choosing to make themselves healthy and fit. The graph compared the leading causes of death for Americans in 1900 ... to the leading causes of death in 1996. Here's what the graph showed:

In 1900, the leading cause of death was tuberculosis, followed by dysentery ... influenza ... small pox ... and pneumonia. In 1996, the leading cause of death was heart disease ... followed by stroke ... cancer ... diabetes ... and emphysema.

I want you to read the list from 1900 again so it will really sink in:

Tuberculosis.

Dysentery.

Influenza.

Small pox.

Pneumonia.

How many Americans do you think die from these diseases today? If you eliminated pneumonia, *the answer might be fewer than a hundred in the whole country!*

Deaths Related to Lifestyle Choices

Now, check out the 1996 list one more time:

Heart disease.

Stroke.

Cancer.

Diabetes.

Emphysema.

Do you see a pattern here? Every one of the modern-day leading causes of death in America could be greatly reduced by changing our habits.

Did you know that one out of every three Americans smokes

cigarettes? Did you know that one out of every three Americans could be classified as clinically obese? Do you think America, as a whole, would become healthier and fitter if all the overweight people lost a few pounds ... and all the cigarette smokers quit? Absolutely!

Here's the point. Advances in medicine have blessed the vast majority of Americans with the *opportunity* to live long, healthy, pain-free lives. Yet millions of Americans are abusing that blessing by regularly eating junk food and sitting on the couch watching the "boob tube" instead of exercising. These are the same people who expect Medicare to pay for the pills to lower their blood pressure .... the same people who expect Medicaid to cover the costs of their open-heart surgery.

Oh, sure, life can be cruel, and sometimes people get sick through no fault of their own. And we all feel for those people. But when people make lifestyle choices that plunge them headlong into sickness, they're intentionally throwing their lives out of balance. If you can't quit smoking for yourself ... if you can't lose weight for yourself ... *do it for your family! Do it for your friends!* They don't want to see you suffer from an illness or die before your time!

That's why I remind people, *"When you've got your health, you've got just about everything."* Choose good health. Choose longevity. Most of all, choose balance.

Friends

Okay, we've talked about the first three F's, that is, *Faith ... Family ...* and *Fitness*. Now it's time to move on to the fourth F — *Friends*.

The great American statesman William Penn once remarked that *"Friendship is a union of spirits."* And I'd have to agree that the phrase "a union of spirits" is a pretty accurate description of what happens when two people connect in such a special, magical way that they become friends.

But I'm not really too concerned that you understand *what friendship is*. I'm more concerned that you understand *how important friendship is* to balancing YOUR LIFE — and *how important friendship is* to helping your friends balance THEIR LIVES, too.

Friends Are Like Ballast

To use the analogy of a ship at sea, your friends are the ballast that keeps your ship on an even course. In case you don't know, ballast is what they call the big rocks or bricks that are loaded onto cargo ships to make sure the boat is stable and sits level in the water.

When you say to your friends, "Level with me," you're asking them to be truthful ... you're asking them to give it to you straight. In effect, you're asking them to act as ballast so you can sit upright in the water, instead of listing to one side or the other.

Unlike your relatives, you choose your friends, don't you? So friendship is a very special kind of relationship because *it's strictly voluntary. It's a matter of choice, not chance.* Because friends have such a dramatic influence on our lives, we have a personal responsibility to choose them VERY carefully. Very carefully, indeed.

Choose Your Friends Carefully

I mentioned earlier in this book that one of my mother's favorite sayings was this one: *"Tell me who you hang out with, and I'll tell you who you are."* I love that saying because it is packed with common sense and wisdom.

If you hang out with successful businesspeople, most likely it's because you're successful in business — or soon will be. You hang out with bank robbers, there's a better than even chance you have robbed — or soon will rob — a bank. You hang out with people who have a great attitude, most likely you've got a great attitude, too.

That's why the first step in treating a person addicted to alcohol or drugs is to counsel them to stop hanging out with so-called "friends" who encouraged their addiction in the first place. "Tell me who you hang out with and I'll tell you who you are," right?

Before an addict can tell you he's NOT *really* an addict, he's got to quit hanging out with addicts. It's only common sense!

The point is this: Friendship is a crucial spoke in our wheel of balance. *And it's the only one we have total control over!* We can't choose our parents ... we can't always choose the kind of health we are in ... and we can't always choose the state of our finances.

But we can — without any reservations — choose our friends! We have total control over who we hang out with ... We have total control over who we counsel with ... We have total control over who we celebrate with when fortune smiles on us ... And we have total control over who we cry with in our moments of despair.

> *"I don't want to be a millionaire. I just want to live like one."*
>
> — Toots Shore

Here's the long and short of it: You are captain of your own ship. You decide which people will act as ballast to keep you on an even keel.

If the ballast gets too heavy to one side, you may have to throw it overboard to save the ship. Or you may have to add new ballast from time to time to keep you on course. But one thing's certain. It would be a foolish captain, indeed, who chose to go down with a sinking ship rather than make adjustments to the ballast!

Finances

Now let's take a look at the final F of the Five F's — *Finances*. Let me preface this discussion by saying that the final F of a balanced life could just as easily have stood for the word "Freedom" instead of the word "Finances." I say that because, in my mind, they're one and the same.

Everyone knows that money itself isn't what has value to us. It's what money can BUY that has value to us. As the legendary Toots Shore used to say, *"I don't want to be a millionaire. I just want to live like one."*

Well, how do millionaires live? Let's see ...

They come and go as they please.

They live just about anywhere they want to live.

They hire people to do the time-consuming things they don't want to do, like cleaning and cooking and mowing the yard.

Which allows millionaires to do what they want ... when they want — like playing golf ... going on vacations ... starting a new business ... growing an existing business ... donating to charity ... reading ... or jetting to New York for a new Broadway play.

Money Is Freedom

Are you beginning to see the point? Money is freedom. Freedom from hunger ... freedom from dead-end jobs ... freedom from tedious chores ... freedom from sending your kids to lousy schools ... freedom from anxiety about making the mortgage payment ... freedom from feeling sick and tired of being sick and tired. Most of all, money is the freedom to make your own choices, rather than to have someone else make them for you!

> *"Do not let what you cannot do interfere with what you can do."*
>
> — *John Wooden*

Look, it's really pretty simple. How can you add balance to your life if you're busy working three dead-end jobs just to make ends meet? How can you add balance to your life when you're forced to live off a meager Social Security check during your retirement years?

The answer is, you can't have balance if your financial house is falling down around you! It's like the old saying, "If your outgo exceeds your income, then your upkeep will be your downfall."

This isn't the place to tell you how to earn money or to save for your retirement. My purpose isn't to tell you *how to make* money. Rather, my purpose is to remind you of the important role that money plays in bringing balance to YOU, INC. — and ultimately, how a balanced life can dramatically increase your fair market value!

What Happens to Millionaires Without Balance

There you have it, the Five F's for Balancing your life: *Faith ... Family ... Fitness ... Friends ...* and *Finances*.

I'd like to conclude this discussion with a quick story that proves beyond a shadow of a doubt just how important balance is in our lives.

In 1923, nine of the world's most successful financiers met at a swanky hotel in Chicago to discuss the economy. These nine men were the richest of the rich. Among those present at the roundtable meeting was the president of the New York Stock Exchange ... the president of the world's largest steel company ... the president of the world's largest electric company .... the president of the world's largest gas company ... and the head of the world's largest monopoly.

Fast forward 25 years to 1948. What do you think had happened to the nine men who had such enormous power and wealth a few years back ... but lacked balance in their lives? Here's a quick summary of their fates:

Three of the nine men committed suicide.

Three of the nine men died broke.

Two of the nine men served time in prison.

One of the nine men was declared legally insane.

Balance Is Essential!

In short, nine out of the nine died unhappy ... broke ... disgraced ... or insane. Every one of these nine men learned how to make money. But not one of them learned the *value of balance*. This story proves that balance isn't just important to your well-being.

Balance, my friend, is *essential!*

• • •

PRINCIPLE 10:
Change — or Be Changed

It's hard for me to get used to these changing times.
I can remember when the air was clean and sex was dirty.
— George Burns

I'd like to open our discussion of change with a story that appeared in the *Wall Street Journal*. The story was about Vickie Barsczak, a city employee who earned about $15 an hour reading electric meters.

Vickie had just lost her job at the Kansas City Power and Light Company because the company had installed newly developed "automatic readers" in the city's 420,000 electric meters.

You see, the automatic reader does the same thing that Vickie did at a fraction of the cost. And its calculations are more accurate ... it doesn't call in sick ... it doesn't join unions ... and it doesn't demand a pension plan. It just keeps on ticking and reporting electric usage to a computer in the central office.

The computer translates the usage into a monthly fee, and then prints out a bill for each customer. Because Kansas City Power and Light Company no longer needed Vickie to read their meters, Vickie lost her $32,000-per-year job. And it's just a matter of time before the remaining 35,000 meter readers nationwide will have their jobs replaced by the automatic reader.

The Changing Job Market

This particular article was about advancing technology forcing Vickie the Meter Reader out of her job. But it could just have easily been about Vickie the Telephone Operator ... or Vickie the Bank

Teller ... or Vickie the Assembly Line Worker ... or Vickie the Ticket Agent ... or Vickie the Whatever She Does and Wherever She Works.

You see, thousands of hard-working Vickie's and Vic's of the world have jobs that are being threatened by the "C-Word," as in CHANGE. You can call it technology ... or you can call it automation ... but the result is always the same: CHANGE! Fast and furious ... cold and calculating ... here-today, gone-tomorrow CHANGE.

Change Is Not an Option

In our hearts we feel sorry for the all the Vickie's and Vic's — all the hard-working Americans whose jobs are being replaced by technology and automation. But the truth of the matter is, we can't stop change. The truth of the matter is, we can't even slow it down.

As Bill Gates put it, *"Change is not an optional thing. We cannot vote and say we want to stop it. In fact, we are changing faster than ever before. But part of the United States' strength is that it has embraced change."*

In a nutshell, Gates is saying "change ... or be changed." Because change is not an option, we might as well take advantage of change by embracing it, instead of waiting for change to take advantage of us!

Two Frogs in a Pan of Hot Water

It's like the story about a couple of frogs that were dropped into two pans of water sitting on a stove. The first frog was dropped into a pan of hot water, and he immediately reacted to the heat by jumping out of the pan.

The second frog was placed into a pan of cold water. The burner beneath the pan was turned on low ... then the heat was gradually increased so that the temperature of the water rose only a degree at a time. Change was occurring, but because it was gradual, the frog ignored it. He stayed in the pan until the temperature reached boiling! Needless to say, that frog is history!

The moral of the story is change ... or be changed: The first frog *changed.* He jumped out of the pan and hopped away to croak another day. But the second frog *was changed!* He stayed in the water ignoring — or perhaps denying — the gradual change in the water temperature until his goose, so to speak, was cooked!

External vs. Internal Changes

This story vividly illustrates the two fundamental kinds of changes: The first kind of changes are the ones we have little or no control over. I call them *external changes.* Generally speaking, external changes would be changes in the world around us, like the economy or advances in technology.

In the frog story, neither frog had control over the temperature of the water — nor whether or not they even wanted to be in the water. Both frogs were at the mercy of external changes.

Internal Changes

The second kind of changes are the ones we DO have control over — that is, the changes in how we respond to external changes. I call these *internal changes.* Internal changes would include changes in our attitude ... changes in our diet and our exercise program ... changes in our education, and so on.

In the frog story, both frogs had control over whether to stay in the water ... or whether to jump out! The first frog chose to do exactly that — he jumped out of the hot water and it saved his life. The second frog chose to ignore the warning signs — and he paid for that choice with his life!

> *"A man is not old until regrets take the place of dreams."*
>
> —John Barrymore

There are obvious parallels between the story of the two frogs and what is happening in the world around us — and what each of us needs to do in order to survive, much less to prosper, in the coming decades.

Changes Occurring Faster Than Ever

For most of the world's history, change has occurred very, very slowly. The Stone Age lasted tens of thousands of years. The Middle Ages lasted a thousand years, well into the 15th century. But change started accelerating as we neared the 20th century.

From the 1850s to the 1970s, the Industrial Age hit full stride, and change came fast and furious, especially in America. Just look at a decade-by-decade list of the technological breakthroughs that quickly evolved from novelties to necessities during the 20th century.

> *"Change is not an optional thing. We cannot vote and say we want to stop it. In fact, we are changing faster than ever before. But part of the United States' strength is that it has embraced change."*
>
> *— Bill Gates*

In 1910, automobiles and tractors started rolling off the assembly lines.

In the 1920s, radios were all the rage.

In the 1930s, telephone sales exploded.

In the 1940s, commercial air travel became affordable.

In the 1950s, televisions took over our living rooms.

In the 1960s, the first industrial robot was introduced.

And in the early 1970s, the personal computer moved computing from the main frame to Main Street.

The demand for these innovations kept the smokestack industries working overtime, and the Industrial Age looked to be healthy ... wealthy ... and wise.

Ironically, it is these very same innovations — the car ... the radio ... the telephone ... the commercial airliner ... the TV ... the industrial robot ... and the PC — that are contributing to the demise of the Industrial Age while simultaneously ushering in the Information Age, an age of unprecedented change and frequent technological breakthroughs.

If you think you've seen a lot of changes in the 20th century, hang on to your hat, because the changes that we'll witness during the Information Age will roar past the changes in the Industrial Age like an Indy 500 race car past a Model T Ford!

Mega-Trends of Change

To better illustrate how fast things are changing in the Information Age, I'd like to list some mega-trends that will boggle your mind. Check out just a few of the mega-trends that spell good news for consumers:

Mega-trend 1: Information is expanding:
Today there are 3,700 more magazines than there were in the 1950s.

Mega-trend 2: Entertainment is exploding:
In the 1970s, there were only three television networks. In the near future there will be 500 or more!

Mega-trend 3: Products are expanding:
In 1976, the typical supermarket carried 9,000 products. Only 15 years later, the local supermarket was carrying 30,000 products!

Mega-trend 4: Personal computers are cheaper and more powerful than ever before:
The first computer, named ENIAC, was introduced in 1946. It cost half a million dollars, weighed 30 tons and filled a room as big as a two-car garage. Today, one dime-sized silicon chip costing a couple hundred dollars has the capacity to easily outperform ENIAC!

Isn't it amazing the number of conveniences and choices available to us in the Information Age? Five hundred TV stations! ... Thirty thousand products and counting! WOW!

Some Disturbing Job Trends

Unfortunately, there's a downside to the Information Age — as many American workers are all too aware. Unfortunately, technology closes as many doors as it opens. Here are some disturbing job trends that prove my point:

Disturbing Job Trend 1: Manufacturing jobs are declining:

In 1950, nearly three out of every four Americans worked in production or manufacturing. Today, about one in ten Americans works in a factory.

Disturbing Job Trend 2: Firing is in, hiring is out:

In the 1950s, every major industry was hiring. In the 1990s, one out of every three workers was laid off.

Disturbing Job Trend 3: Job security is a thing of the past:

The average American worker will have 10 to 12 different jobs in 4 to 5 different career areas during their lifetime.

Disturbing Job Trend 4: Permanent jobs are being replaced by part-time workers.

In 1995, a fast-growing temporary-employment agency called Manpower Services surged past General Motors to become the biggest employer in the U.S.

What does all this mean to you and me? It means that we are just now entering an era of unimaginable changes in our world as we make the transition from the Old Economy of the Industrial Age ... to the New Economy of the Information Age.

Change: Friend or Foe?

Some of those changes are going to benefit millions of Americans in the long run, such as breakthroughs in science and medicine. Other changes will hurt millions of Americans working in traditional manufacturing jobs, as global competition and automation whittle away at their jobs.

Warren Bennis, a distinguished professor of business administration at USC, describes how automation and technology will transform manufacturing this way:

"The factory of the future will have only two employees, a man and a dog. The man will be there to feed the dog. The dog will be there to keep the man from touching the equipment."

Bennis' factory of the future may be an exaggeration, but it certainly drives home the main point of this program. That is, good jobs will be scarce ... and life will be rough ... for Americans who can't — or won't — make the paradigm shift from thinking of themselves as employees ... to thinking of themselves as YOU, INC.

The Bright Side of Automation

Let's take another look at the opening story about Vickie the Meter Reader. At first glance, it might seem like Vickie is getting a raw deal — just one more sad story about a human losing ground to ever-increasing technology.

But if you look beneath the surface, the issue isn't just about thousands of meter readers losing their jobs. It's also about the thousands of *opportunities* created by the installation of the automatic reader.

> *"The factory of the future will have only two employees, a man and a dog. The man will be there to feed the dog. The dog will be there to keep the man from touching the equipment."*
>
> — *Warren Bennis*

Here's a brief scenario that illustrates the positive side of changes brought about by technology. If every city in America converted to the automatic reader, can you imagine what that would entail?

Thousands of people will be hired to manufacture the automatic readers ... thousands more workers will be needed to install them ... each city will need to buy and install the computer software to convert the readings into monthly billing statements ... The manufacturers of the software and the automatic reader will need to hire marketing people to design their packaging ... advertising people to get the word out ... salespeople to call on customers ... and so on.

The story about Vickie the Meter Reader is a classic example of what happens when the world shifts from the Old Economy based on capital and manual labor ... to the new economy based on technology and creative solutions.

It's too bad that Vickie the employee lost her job. But won't it be wonderful when Vic the Independent Contractor gets hired to install automatic readers in every home and business in Kansas City?

Vickie's Loss Is Vic's Gain

The truth of the matter is that Vickie's loss is Vic's gain. And that, my friend, is the way free enterprise works, like it or not. And if you're anything like me, you'll like it — love it, in fact — because the alternative to free enterprise is something called communism.

> *"Ignoring the facts doesn't make them any less true."*
>
> —Aldous Huxley

No one said that a market-driven economy like ours was Utopia. There's no question that a lot of Americans will have problems making the transition from the Industrial Age to the Information Age. But there's no turning back the clock. Wishing for the good old days of working nine to five and enjoying guaranteed annual pay raises won't bring them back. For the vast majority of workers, those days are dead and gone forever.

Two Amazing Examples of Change

To illustrate how pervasive change is in our society today, take a look at these eye-opening statistics: Did you know that today there are more Americans building personal computers than cars? Considering the automobile had a 75-year head start on the PC industry, that's a pretty telling statistic, wouldn't you agree?

Here's another one: Did you know that Microsoft's Windows '95 manual required the largest single order for paper in the history of the world? Amazingly, the Windows program had only been on the market five years prior to that order! When a young, high-tech product can create such a huge market in a few short years, it's undeniable evidence of how fast things will change during the Information Age.

Shift from Old Economy to New Economy

Nuala Beck, author of *Shifting Gears: Thriving in the New Economy*, has this to say about the shift from the Old Economy to the New Economy:

> *"The New Economy became a factor in 1981. That's when, statistically, we saw the old industries that had been in the driver's seat hitting their peak, and the new industries growing larger than the old ones.*
>
> *"In 1981, the IBM PC moved onto desktops. Fax machines appeared in offices. From 1981 onward, we have been involved in a massive paradigm shift that has impacted every company, every industry, every individual. Many people — including experts — are still waiting for the new, technology-based economy to emerge. But it's already here and has been for at least a decade."*

We Can't Ignore the Facts

I've said it before and I'll say it again: *Ignoring the facts doesn't make them any less true.* And the fact is we're living in a fast-changing world. Whether we like it or not, we're like the two frogs in a pan of water. We do NOT have a lot of control over the external changes in our world, like the shift from the Old Economy to the New Economy.

What we do have control over, however, is how we REACT to those external changes. As I see it, the key is to dramatically improve the fair market value of YOU, INC. so that you can take advantage of change, instead of change taking advantage of you!

The great Czech novelist Franz Kafka once said, *"In a fight between you and the world, bet on the world."* Well, the world is changing.

The old smokestack jobs are going the way of the dinosaurs, while new information-driven jobs are springing up all over the place. What we all need to do is to "bet on the world" by changing ourselves ... instead of trying to change the world by fighting it.

For Things to Get Better, YOU Have to Get Better!

Changing yourself is what we'll be discussing for the balance of this chapter. If you are serious about wanting to succeed in the years ahead, you're going to have to make some changes in YOU, INC., that's for sure.

As management guru Tom Peters put it, and I quote: *"Change is disruptive .... But it doesn't make any difference. You gotta do it anyway. We're in an era where, literally, to learn to love change is the only survival course."*

If you are sincere about wanting to dramatically improve your fair market value, you have to get better! And it only stands to reason that in order for you to get better, you must make some changes in your life.

> *"In a fight between you and the world, bet on the world."*
>
> — *Franz Kafka*

That's why I always say, *"For things to get better, you have to get better. For things to change, you have to change."*

You know, when it's all said and done, wouldn't you agree that most of us are after the same thing? Wouldn't you agree that we all want to own our own home and drive a nice car? ... we all want freedom to come and go as we please ... we all want financial security ... we all want good health for ourselves and our families ... and we want our kids to get a good education so they can grow up to get their fair share of the American Dream.

If those are some of the things you want out of life, but you're headed down a road that's not taking you there, you've got to change your direction or your approach, right? In the words of the famous motivational speaker Jim Rohn: *"If you want your next five years to be a whole lot better than your last five years, you've got to make some changes in your life."*

A Story of Tragedy ... and Triumph

I'd like to wrap up this section with a story that perfectly illustrates what can happen to people who are willing to make positive changes in their lives — and what can happen to people who refuse to change.

The story is about two brothers named Michael and Chris. Michael and Chris were both born in the early 1960s and grew up in a mostly black neighborhood in Richmond, California, right outside of San Francisco.

Both boys were well behaved in school and brought home mostly A's on their report cards all through grade school.

But coming from a working-class family with eight children, money was always tight, so the boys often had to go without. In fact, things were so tight, the two growing boys were often hungry.

Brothers in Crime

So they did what many boys do when they're hungry and have no food — they stole. From the time they were five until they were well out of high school, the boys stole. They stole crackers from the cupboard in the middle of the night ... they stole cookies from the grocery store ... and they stole sandwiches from the sandwich shop.

If it wasn't nailed down and was worth something, Michael and Chris would find a way to steal it. They even stole money from their parents from time to time. But more often than not, they stole to satisfy their hunger.

When it was time for Michael and Chris to attend high school, they were bused across town to Kennedy High School. It was during high school that something happened that made Chris decide to change his behavior. At the end of his freshman year in high school, Chris had received three A's and three F's on his report card — the first time he had failed anything in school.

Choosing to Succeed Instead of Fail

Because Kennedy High School only allowed three failures over four years, one more F and Chris would be kicked out of school. That's when he made up his mind to change. Years later Chris would recall that defining moment in his life with these words:

"I sat outside my house at the beginning of that summer knowing that I was letting my chance slip away. One more F and I'd be just another high school dropout, hanging around the neighborhood, hoping to get on with the county or to get into the service.

"At the time I didn't know my brother Rusty would end up in prison ... or that my brother Harold would die without having seen much of the world. I certainly didn't know what would happen to Michael. I only knew that I had to get out of there. I wanted to see San Francisco every day, to pick out my own clothes, drive my own car, and be whatever a man could hope to be, not just a black man, not just a man from the flats of Richmond. I wanted no limitations. I wanted to be whatever a man could hope to be."

Chris' decision to change his behavior wasn't an easy one. He took a lot of grief from his friends for choosing to excel in school, instead of squeaking by with C's and D's. But that decision to change took him in an entirely different direction from his brother Michael, who resisted changing his unproductive behavior.

Chris went on to graduate from high school ... graduate from college ... and graduate from law school. For 15 years he worked as a Deputy District Attorney in Los Angeles, California, prosecuting murderers, drug dealers, gang members and crooked cops. Today Chris is better known as Christopher. You probably recognize him by his full name — Christopher Darden, one of the lead prosecutors in the trial of the century, the O. J. Simpson trial!

The Fate of the Older Brother

What became of Christopher's brother, Michael? After high school

Michael joined the army and returned to his hometown shortly after his tour of duty. Back in Richmond, Michael continued his pattern of anti-social behavior — hustling in the streets ... and stealing to support himself and a growing drug habit. On November 29, 1995, Michael Darden died at the age of 42 ... from AIDS.

The Choice Is Yours, and Yours Alone

This story of triumph and tragedy serves to remind us that when it's all said and done, who we are and what we become is determined by the choices we make.

We can choose to get better ... or we can choose to get bitter. Whether we make those choices to improve at age 14, like Christopher Darden ... or at age 64, like Colonel Sanders, those choices have the power to dramatically increase our value in virtually everything we do.

That's what the saying "change ... or be changed" is all about. Christopher Darden changed. He changed from being a criminal ... to prosecuting criminals.

He changed his attitude from being angry and sullen ... to being open and accepting.

He changed from an underachiever ... to an honor student who took responsibility for his grades and his education.

He changed from a disillusioned teen-ager with low self-esteem ... to an optimistic young man determined to turn his dreams into reality.

His brother Michael, on the other hand, was changed. He was changed by grinding poverty ... he was changed by the code of the streets ... he was changed by illegal drugs ... and finally, he was changed by an insidious disease.

Making the Tough Choices

Christopher Darden made the tough choices ... he made the changes in his life that helped him accomplish his dreams.

His brother Michael, on the other hand, took the easy way out — or at least what he thought was the easy way out. He kept hanging around the same group of loser friends ... he kept practicing the same self-destructive habits. As a result of the changes they did or did not make, both men chose their fates: Christopher chose to became a successful prosecutor. And Michael chose to become just another sad story of the streets.

Either Way, You Pay

The sobering truth is, "Either way, you pay!" The truth is the price that Michael paid for refusing to change was much higher than the price that Christopher paid for seeking to change.

I'd like to think that Michael didn't die in vain. I'd like to think that by hearing this story, some people will finally understand the profound importance of making positive, productive changes in their lives.

When it's all said and done, you have a choice.

You can choose to become Michael.

Or you can choose to become Christopher.

You can continue to do the things that will lead to frustration and unhappiness.

Or you can make the changes that help you get what you want most out of life.

Don't choose to become like so many people who COULD HAVE *become a millionaire* ... or who COULD HAVE *become happier* ... or who COULD HAVE *become healthier* ... or who COULD HAVE *made a contribution* — but didn't.

Start making the changes you need to make TODAY ... so that you can become the person you want to become TOMORROW!

• • •

SECTION 3

· · ·

Conclusion

All the mistakes I ever made were when I wanted to say "no" but said "yes" instead.
— Moss Hart
playwright and humorist

CONCLUSION:
Choice, Not Chance, Determines Your Destiny

What lies behind us and what lies before us are
tiny matters compared to what lies within us.
— Ralph Waldo Emerson

R J. Wrigley, the founder and president of Wrigley Chewing Gum, was one of the first businessmen to take full advantage of advertising.

While his competitors were spending thousands of dollars on advertising, Wrigley was spending millions. In the 1940s it was hard to open a newspaper or drive by a billboard without seeing a promotion for Wrigley Chewing Gum.

During a commercial flight to an important board meeting, a passenger interrupted Wrigley as he was preparing for the meeting and asked, *"Mr. Wrigley, perhaps you could answer a question that has been bothering me for a long time: Why do you continue to advertise your gum so widely when your company already sells more gum than all your competitors combined?"*

Wrigley looked up from his paperwork, scowled at the man and replied, *"I keep advertising for the same reason the pilot of this airplane keeps the engines running after we are already in the air."*

You Are the Pilot of Your Own Destiny

Just think about his answer for a moment, because the principle is the same whether you're talking about advertising ... flying a plane ... or growing as a person.

If you want to arrive at your destination, you have to keep the engines running.

My objective during our time together is to provide you with the fuel that will help you to keep the engines of YOU, INC. running smoothly and efficiently.

You'll need to refuel between flights ... you'll need to check in for regular maintenance ... and you may have to undergo major repairs from time to time. But never forget that you are the pilot of your own destiny. And the decision to keep the engines running — or to stay parked on the ground — is yours, and yours alone.

Think — YOU, INC.!

We've covered a lot of material in this book, so let's take a moment right now to review the central themes and key messages we've talked about so far:

First and foremost, let me remind you that the main theme behind the YOU, INC. program is for you to *understand the importance* of expanding your personal paradigm so that you can discover the CEO within. In short, you must remember that you are founder, president and 100 percent stockholder in YOU ... so you've got to Think — YOU, INC.!

The cornerstone of YOU, INC. is that the same principles that successful companies use to increase their fair market value and generate millions of dollars in profits can be applied to the lives of average people — people just like you and me — to dramatically increase *our value*.

Instead of limiting our potential by thinking of ourselves in traditional, narrowly defined ways that we've been taught — such as "I'm Emma the Employee" or "I'm Henry, Husband and Father" — we MUST expand the boundaries of our thinking so that we begin to think and act like a successful company. Again, Think — YOU, INC.!

Invest in Your Hidden Assets

Let me ask you a question: Would you want to invest in a company that had millions of dollars in unused assets stored in huge vaults? Of course not. You'd want that company to put those under-used assets to work earning even more money, wouldn't you? If the money were just lying in a corner gathering dust, it might as well not exist, for all the good it's doing.

The same can be said for YOU, INC. If you have talents and abilities that you aren't using, it's like sticking money in a safe deposit box, closing the door and then forgetting where you put the key.

In my estimation, the person born without talent is better off than the person who squanders it, because the squanderer is abusing his gifts!

Unused talents and abilities can't help you grow.

Unused talents and abilities can't increase your value.

Unused talents and abilities can't do anything but weigh you down with guilt.

Self-limiting thoughts and actions are the twin enemies of our potential. As a wise person once said, *"When you put fences around people, you get sheep."* Well, the same thing happens to people whether someone else puts fences around them — which is what happens in a system like communism ... or whether people put fences around themselves. Either way, self-limited humans become docile sheep instead of the happy ... fulfilled ... prosperous people that God designed us to become.

I look at it this way. If God wanted us to put our heads down and graze, He would have made us sheep in the first place. But God designed us humans to stand upright so that we could reach toward the heavens and gaze at the stars! You can break through the self-limiting fences by understanding ... applying ... and living the 10 principles of YOU, INC.

EQ Revisited

Early in the introduction, we talked about the concept of emotional intelligence — our EQ — as opposed to our intellectual intelligence — better known as IQ. We learned two important things about EQ that bear repeating. One, up to 80 percent of our success in life can be attributed to EQ, not IQ; and two, unlike IQ, which is pretty much fixed at birth, we can improve our EQ virtually anytime during our lives. Which means average people, like you and me, can lead above-average lives if we are willing to take responsibility for our personal growth.

Increasing Your Fair Market Value

We've also discussed the concept of value and how we can dramatically increase the value of YOU, INC. The fair market value for people with minimum skills and minimum experience is — you guessed it — minimum wage. By the same token, people who start working for the minimum wage can dramatically increase their earning power as they dramatically increase their value.

A Case Study of Increased Value

A successful businesswoman named Cheri Dohse wrote a guest column for *USA Today* that perfectly illustrates the concept of increased value. Dohse was a single mother earning $2.90 per hour as a part-time cashier when she started working for Cousins Submarine Shop in 1981.

> *"When you put fences around people, you get sheep."*
>
> *—Anonymous*

Within months she received a raise. Over the next 15 years, she held just about every job available at Cousins. Because she worked hard, had a great attitude and was willing to learn, Cousins officials encouraged Dohse to enter their management training program.

She rose through the ranks to become a district manager of eight Cousins shops in Milwaukee, overseeing 300 employees. One of her jobs today is to train future managers at Cousins, helping them move from low-paying jobs to a profitable career path, just as she had done. Her goal is to one day own her own Cousins franchise.

Stories like this one are played out thousands and thousands of times every day all across this great country of ours. There are a lot of self-motivated people who figure out through trial and error how to dramatically increase their fair market value. What I've tried to do with the YOU, INC. program is to give people a head start by helping them understand the principles that the Cheri Dohse's of the world use to increase their value.

Reviewing the 10 Principles

Let's take a moment to briefly review the 10 principles:

Principle Number 1: *Take responsibility* encourages us to take control of our lives by taking responsibility for our actions ... our happiness ... our successes ... our health ... and our finances.

Principle Number 2: *Dare to Dream* reminds us that our dreams are the blueprints of our future successes ... and that the people who achieve the biggest successes are always the biggest dreamers.

Principle Number 3: *The Power of Belief* discusses the importance of replacing I CAN'T thinking — what I call "stinkin' thinkin'" — with I CAN thinking.

Principle Number 4: *The Courage to Take Action* reminds us that small, consistent actions can yield huge dividends ... and that it takes daily courage and discipline to overcome the two biggest enemies of action — procrastination and excuses.

Principle Number 5: *Attitude Is Everything* confirms the following observation by W. Clement Stone: "There is little difference in people. But that little difference makes a big difference. The little difference is attitude. The big difference is whether it is positive or negative."

Principle Number 6: *Develop Productive Habits* tells us the importance of choosing productive habits that will make us better, rather than unproductive habits that set us up for failure.

Principle Number 7: *Manage Your Emotions* emphasizes the importance of our being in charge of how we feel ... and reminds us that when it comes to emotions, it's either RUN or RUIN — that is, RUN your emotions, or your emotions will RUIN your life!

Principle Number 8: *Prepare for Success* emphasizes the importance of acquiring useful knowledge and refining our skills by attending seminars ... reading books ... listening to tapes ... and associating with positive people.

Principle Number 9: *Balance Your Life* communicates that in order to be complete human beings, we need to balance the Five F's in our lives, that is Faith, Family, Fitness, Friends and Finances.

Principle Number 10: *Change — Or Be Changed* explains that the key to change is making it work for us, instead of against us ... and that we must consciously change and grow as individuals if we are serious about dramatically improving our fair market value.

There you have it. The 10 simple principles to dramatically increase the fair market value of YOU, INC.

Now, throughout this book I've emphasized the power contained in each of these 10 principles to dramatically transform the lives of average people for the better! And throughout this book we've used scores of examples of successful people who have magically transformed their lives by incorporating one or more of these 10 principles.

A Sad But True Story about Underestimated Value

Now I'd like to tell you a very different kind of story ... a sad story about what can happen when people UNDERESTIMATE the fair market value of their talents ... their ideas ... and their creativity.

The story concerns two childhood friends from Cleveland named Jerry Siegel and Joe Shuster.

Jerry was a scrawny, awkward high school student who spent most of his waking hours lost in his daydreams. Like most high school boys, Jerry had a crush on several attractive girls. Unfortunately, they didn't return his crushes. In fact, they didn't even return a glance in his direction.

In Jerry's own words, *"I had crushes on girls who either didn't know I existed ... or didn't care I existed."* As a result of this rejection, Jerry's imagination went into overdrive! He began imagining what the cutest girls in his school would think if he had something special going for him ... like super-human strength or super-powers that allowed him to fly.

Jerry confided his daydreams to his best friend, Joe Shuster, who was experiencing the same kind of rejection in his life. Joe didn't have Jerry's talent for story-telling, but he was an exceptional artist. Joe could draw just about anything and make it look like it was just about to walk off the page.

Together the two outsiders spent hours and hours together. Jerry would think of fantastic stories, and then Joe would illustrate them with his vivid drawings.

Super Hero Is a Hit

The two friends stayed in close touch after graduating from high school. Jerry continued to write ... Joe continued to illustrate ... and eventually, a fictional alter-ego of the two young men began to emerge.

The character possessed super-human powers. Siegel imagined his character as being born on the doomed planet Krypton ... arriving in a spaceship as an infant ... and being discovered and raised by a childless older couple somewhere in the great Midwest. When the boy grew up, he hid his super-powers from others by working as a mild-mannered newspaper reporter.

Joe sketched out the character as fast as Jerry wrote about his adventures. Joe drew him in a vivid blue, ski-tight suit with a bright red cape. Emblazoned on the suit was a crescent containing a big red "S" for the character's name — SUPERMAN.

On Top of the World

Jerry and Joe became more and more excited about their creation with each passing day. By the time the two friends were in their early 20s, they were shopping their illustrated story of Superman to publishers, only to receive a pile of rejection letters.

In March of 1938, the Superman stories landed on the desk of the publisher of DC Comics, who was so impressed he bought the exclusive rights to the Superman character on the spot — and then gave both young men jobs at the company.

It was the spring of 1938, and Jerry and Joe were on top of the

. . . .

world! Here they were, two childhood buddies, only 23 years old, employed full time with the leading publisher of comic books. It was a dream come true!

Super Story with a Sad Ending

Wouldn't it be great if this story ended right here, on this happy note, with two talented young guys starting a successful, profitable career doing what they loved?

Sadly, this is a story about what happens to people who don't fully understand the meaning of value or how to improve it. It's a story of what can happen when people underestimate their fair market value. The rest of the story is heartbreaking.

> *"The most delightful surprise in life is to suddenly recognize your own worth."*
>
> — *Maxwell Maltz*

As we all know, the Superman character became a huge hit with the American public. Since its debut, Superman has generated untold profits from comic book sales ... licensing deals ... television series ... feature films ... the list goes on. The first Superman movie alone made more than $100 million. The monetary value of the Superman character since its inception in 1938 must be well into the billions of dollars.

So, what percentage of that profit do you think Jerry and Joe received? The answer will stun you. Are you ready?

$130. That's it. *One hundred and thirty dollars!*

They signed away their rights to the Superman character worth billions — for a measly $130. That's $65 apiece! That's painful, isn't it? What a waste!

From Bad to Worse

If that's not bad enough, when the character became such a sensation, Jerry and Joe asked DC Comics for a share of the profits. You know what the two friends got for an answer? They were fired.

They not only lost Superman. They lost their jobs!

After a series of lawsuits to recover their creative property failed, the men lived out the rest of their lives in near poverty. Jerry worked as a typist in Los Angeles. Joe worked as a messenger in Manhattan.

In 1978, after the first Superman movie became a box office hit, DC Comics bowed to public pressure and gave each man a $20,000-per-year annuity. In their final years, the two childhood friends lived within blocks of each other in Los Angeles. Joe died broke and alone in 1992. Jerry died nearly penniless only four years later.

Do you think Jerry and Joe would have sold their rights to the Superman character for a measly $130 if they had fully understood the concept of YOU, INC. ... if they had discovered "the CEO within" ... and if they had fully understood the 10 principles that can dramatically increase their fair market value? Not a chance!

Ignorance Cost Them a Fortune

Joe and Jerry were exploited by some savvy businessmen because these life long friends simply didn't know any better. Their ignorance cost them a fortune! Think about it — if they had known what you and I know, you better believe their lives would have taken a much different direction.

The story about Jerry and Joe makes me sad because two young, naive guys got taken to the cleaners because *they did NOT understand how to dramatically increase their fair market value!*

It also makes me sad for the millions of Americans we never hear about who are being exploited because they, too, are under-utilitzing their assets ... underestimating their fair market value ... and selling themselves way too cheap.

Don't Become Another Joe and Jerry

Maxwell Maltz, renowned surgeon and best-selling author, once remarked: *"The most delightful surprise in life is to suddenly recognize your own worth."*

Friends, my sincere wish for you is that the principles in this book give you the knowledge ... the wisdom ... and the understanding to *recognize your own worth!* Because Joe and Jerry failed to recognize their own worth, they spent almost 60 years of their lives trying to recover what was rightfully theirs — IF ONLY THEY HAD RECOGNIZED IT!

Life Is Like a 10-Speed Bike

A humorist once remarked that *"Life is like a 10-speed bike. Most of us have gears we never use."* To verify the truth of that statement, all you have to do is take a glance around you.

For example, we all know childhood friends who were blessed with great athletic ability ... but who have chosen as adults to let their God-given talents go unused while they willingly turn themselves into overweight couch potatoes.

We all know childhood friends who were so full of adventure and passion in their youth ... but who have chosen to become increasingly sullen and bitter as they grow older.

> *"Life is like a 10-speed bike. Most of us have gears we never use."*
>
> —Anonymous

We all know "whiz kids" from high school and college who were always heading up class projects and fund-raisers ... but who as adults traded in their entrepreneurial spirits for a "secure" job they hate.

Do you think those people are using all 10 of their gears? Or do you think they're stuck in low gear because it's easier to turn the pedals? Sure, it may be easier to turn the pedals in low gear, but it's also easier to spin your wheels and get stuck in a rut!

"If I Had My Life to Live Over ..."

Erma Bombeck, the famous humorist and columnist, once wrote a very serious column shortly before she died from a rare kidney disorder. The column was about what she would do differently if she had her life to live over. She gave a long list of small, everyday things she would do differently — before ending her column with a powerful, heartfelt sentiment that nearly brought me to tears. Here's what she said she would do differently if she could live her life over:

"*There would have been more I love you's ... more I'm sorry's ... more I'm listening's .... But mostly, given another shot at life, I would seize every minute of it ... look at it and really see it ... try it on ... live it ... exhaust it ... and never give a minute back until there was nothing left of it.*"

> *"Look inside yourself. You are more than what you have become."*
>
> — *from "The Lion King"*

Sadly, Erma Bombeck won't get another shot at this life. But in a very real sense, Erma Bombeck is giving you and me "another shot at life" by reminding us that we have been given the gift of choice ... and we can, in fact, CHOOSE to live life as she so eloquently described it — *starting right this moment!*

Purpose of YOU, INC.

When it's all said and done, my purpose in the YOU, INC. program is to to offer you the information that will allow you to have all the things in life that you deserve. By understanding the principles we've discussed ... and then by incorporating them into your life, I'm convinced you will improve the quality of your life beyond your wildest dreams.

Look Inside Yourself

I'd like to conclude this book by telling you about an episode from my family's all-time favorite movie, Disney's animated classic — *The Lion King*. The following scene perfectly illustrates not only what YOU, INC. is all about, but more importantly, why you must THINK — YOU, INC. — starting right now!

Near the end of the movie, the young lion king, Simba, is living in exile, trying his best to avoid his responsibilities as an adult by escaping into a life of meaningless leisure.

Simba is finally forced to grow up and face reality when he is confronted by a vision of his late father, King Mufasa. In Simba's vision, King Mufasa challenges his only son to take his rightful place as King of the Pridelands with these words:

"Simba, you have forgotten who you are. Look inside yourself. You are more than what you have become."

YOU ARE MORE THAN WHAT YOU HAVE BECOME!

> *"We don't need more strength or more ability or greater opportunity. What we need is to use what we have."*
>
> — *Basil S. Walsh*

What a powerful statement! And I, for one, think that this message speaks to far more adults in the audience than children. When I look around and see the vast human talent that is being untapped or under-used, it just breaks my heart!

I don't know about you, but I can't think of any fate worse than getting old and sitting in a rocking chair *regretting* the fact that I hadn't lived up to my fullest potential.

How about you? Can you look in the mirror and honestly say you're living up to your fullest potential?

Or are you holding back on your potential ... and holding out on the quality of your life by not being all you can be?

Sadly, too many of us have *"forgotten who we are"* ... and too many of us are *"more than what we have become."*

Don't Squander It!

What I'm talking about here isn't some clever line from an animated movie. This is real. This is serious! You've got to understand that life is not a dress rehearsal!

This is it, my friend — it's showtime!

You're on ... and you're live.

You've got one chance ... so don't squander your life by giving a half-hearted performance! Please, please don't squander your life by putting a fence around yourself.

Just as King Mufasa helped his son Simba to look inside himself so that he would pursue his rightful place as king of the Pridelands ... I sincerely hope that during our time together, I've been able to help you look inside yourself by opening your mind ... and by expanding the way you think of yourself and your place in the world.

Discover Your Full Potential

I challenge you to look inside yourself and discover, once and for all, what you can become.

For I truly believe that once you discover the full value of YOU, INC., you will become not only what you were meant to become ... you will also *become more than you ever dreamed!*

• • •